# Trinity

# Trinity

## Song and Dance God

## ROGER FORSTER

This book is dedicated to Mark Harris, one of my past trainees and a fellow worker in the gospel, whose untiring labours with the computer have never ceased to evoke my admiration and amazement while helping me in the production of this work.

# Foreword

## by Professor Rob George

What's all this business about the Trinity? I have enough trouble being taken seriously by my secular scientific colleagues as a believer in God at all, let alone believing in one that claims to be the one-and-only God, but is in fact three! This just shows how incoherent, arcane and anachronistic Christianity really is, doesn't it? Emphatically no. In fact, it is quite the reverse.

In this third book in his series we find Roger Forster applying, once again, his considerable and uncompromising intellect and scholarship to a cornerstone of our faith: the Trinity. At face value, it is a 'counter-intuition', but within a few pages and relatively little reflection, thoughts and ideas dawn that begin to make a great deal of sense. Those of you who are familiar with his approach will delight in the agility of the ideas and explanations in the following pages as he walks through the arguments for, attractions of and objections to a 'triune God'.

In my own journey, I recall well an evening some years after my conversion when I discovered the Holy Spirit. At a stroke, I realized why I had failed as a Christian thus far; why my belief, based in logic and relying on the intellectual propositions of a Cambridge conversion, seemed so devoid of a heart relationship with God. So was this the immanent God: the power that raised Christ from the dead, the person for whom I was to be a temple? Was this the missing link for those like me? Certainly I had found the power now to change. Simultaneously, of course, I had stumbled into the reality of the Trinity in the absence of a theology or rationality – a bad place for a scientifically trained sceptic. I wasn't satisfied; I had to understand, for our God is reason-able. Like us, He has to follow His own laws of language, logic and coherence. And so for me a new journey began.

It was clear that God must exist: an open-minded view of the moral and philosophical arguments and evidence from science and mathematics drives one indubitably to our Creator (as Sherlock Holmes put it: '. . . when you have exhausted all the possibilities, whatever remains, however improbable, must be the truth'). Equally, it was clear that God must be involved: for to create this universe and then simply to watch from afar is absurd. But for God to intervene in the affairs of humankind and deal adequately with our greatest fears – isolation, death and judgement – requires Him personally to resolve the conflict of truth and freedom. Yet God clearly cannot come down Himself – unless, that is, He is a 'plurality'. So that accounted for the Son. However, the Holy Spirit as the God-with-and-in-us had escaped my tidy and rational, conservative theology for nigh on ten years. The reason, quite simply, was that no one had told me – perhaps because they held the view that the third person of the Trinity was merely an insubstantial Ghost. I hadn't yet gripped the fact that a God of love needed relationship in and through which to bless. It was only after He broke into my consciousness that I saw there must be a whole theology of the Trinity of which I was ignorant, and in true academic fashion I don't hold views without reason. What followed was, and continues to be, a voyage of excitement and discovery as I have found Scripture to respond not only to the needs of daily life, but to any theological, intellectual or moral argument that seeks to stand against it. With respect to the case for the Trinity, you need not wade, as I have, through acres of dense and arid tomes to unearth answers to the superficial counter-intuitions of a plurality within a unity in order to grasp the bones of the conventional arguments. They are all here, and more.

As usual, Roger Forster's starting point for enquiry is Scripture, from which he establishes the biblical credentials of Trinitarianism before demonstrating the philosophical necessity of a plural Godhead and explaining the experiences of believers. Having introduced the subject, he then takes us on an exciting journey through symbols, images and models that will resonate with readers of different traditions and perspectives, while always drawing us back to the source of our revelation, the word of God and the testimony of Jesus. Even biology has a showing in the chapter on the triple helix – it excites me as a clinician to know that the code of life is written in syllables of three. Most stimulating is Forster's boyish excitement at what a Trinity means for us and how Father, Son and Spirit interact to create and reveal the richness of our universe and the unplumbable depths of this triumvirate source of love.

Some chapter headings will tease with the prospect of their contents, and I for one find them all to be most satisfying. Stay with those sections that use unfamiliar concepts. For example, spend time understanding why a plural God is a philosophically logical necessity; appreciate how pervasive Greek thought has been in forming the premises we bring to our Western theology, and enjoy the fascinating weave of thesis and antithesis that forms the section on *The Opponents*. Here Roger Forster verges on the dialectical, but remains resolute and persuasive on the historical legitimacy of Trinitarianism.

Forster pulls the work together with an electric practical application of Trinitarian theology to what are arguably the principal impediments to the *eschaton* – the last days: disunity, inequality and illegitimate spiritual power. The book culminates in a chapter on Trinitarian worship and St Patrick's prayer.

Devote time to this book. It does justice to one of the most important and coherent planks of our faith: that our God is a Father who loves us, a Son who saves us and a Spirit who helps us, and that they are so mixed together in divine relationship as practically to be one – such is the 'Song and Dance God'.

Rob George MA MD FRCP FRSM
King's College London,
Summer 2015

# Preface to the Second Edition

The first edition of *Trinity* sold out very quickly. This was no doubt for many reasons. First, many Christians avoid worshipping and meditating about the Trinity due to fearing its complexity. Consequently any hope of getting past this barrier is welcomed by sincere believers. Secondly, with growing numbers of encounters with Muslims, and reports of Muslim increase in the UK and the English speaking world, there arise many embarrassments in explaining what we mean concerning our God's unity in diversity, namely the Trinity. Thirdly, aggressive 'new atheism' dismisses our doctrine of plurality in the Godhead as irrational and leaves some Christians retreating into mysticism rather than trying to meet their attackers on their own rational ground.

For all of the above reasons I have been under pressure to produce a second edition of my book with just a few additions concerning the rise of trinitarianism out of the strictest monotheistic Jewish society of the first century.

The book is re-launched with prayers for the acceptance, enlightenment, and strengthening of its readers, by our wonderful Trinitarian God.

Roger Forster
London, Spring 2015

# Contents

# Introduction

The Trinity, that is, the description by God of Himself as being 'Three in One', is an extremely important subject for theology. It is one of the doctrines unique to Christianity, and as such it is often attacked by proponents of other philosophies, and even at times questioned by some Christians themselves. Christian ideas about the Trinity have changed, developed and emerged in many different varieties over the centuries since the birth of the Church. This development of ideas should not make us uneasy or cause us to question our biblical basis for the doctrine – dialogue and debate are the human processes whereby truth can break forth from the Scriptures and shine into our current situations, giving greater coherence and, therefore, ever-increasing authority.

Let me give you an analogy that you may find helpful. Science could be called 'humankind's product derived from the *data* of the universe that God established at creation'. (Science literally means 'knowledge'. What we ordinarily call 'science' is properly called 'natural science' – the knowledge we have through studying the physical world and discovering the laws that it follows. Other sciences include social science, medical science, philosophy, theology, and so forth. Throughout the book, unless stated otherwise, I am taking science to mean the physical and

1

biological sciences.) Humankind goes to the data of the universe – that which cannot be changed – and we observe it, measure it and probe into it as far as we can, until we develop a 'science' or knowledge which explains why things work the way they do. These are not all unchangeable truths, of course, for as time goes by humankind discovers new things in the universe and so science keeps developing. For example, we find that the earth is round, and not flat as we previously supposed, and that the earth revolves around the sun, rather than the sun around the earth, as was once assumed to be the case. Thus, the study of natural science is continually growing and changing as new empirical (measurable) knowledge modifies theories and deepens our understanding of *how* things work. Sometimes we build on certain models until we find that they do not fit the data any more, and then we discard the models and start all over again. That is how all sciences (natural, medical, social, and so on) are *humankind's product from God's given data.*

Theology develops in a similar way. Theology is also a science, but it draws on a much broader body of data than the material world. It comprises humankind's attempts to understand the data of Scripture, and from it to build a coherent model by which we may grasp the truth about who God is, and how He relates to His creation. Theology endeavours to find a model in which each part fits with the next, and no part contradicts another. In other words, like any science or theory of knowledge, it must strive continually towards complete coherence and is therefore continually growing and developing. We are not necessarily discovering new *revelations* all the time, for we have the basic data set out for us in the Scriptures. Theology is the exercise of the human mind around the 'givens' of God, with the goal of gaining a deeper and greater *understanding* of who it is that we are worshipping.

Now, science is a noble activity, but it has sometimes dominated our thinking and become a god in its own right. At the heart of modernism is the god of the natural sciences, so that we worship the empirical method and only believe in the things that can be measured or investigated from our material surroundings. (Empiricism is a theory of knowledge whose claim is that for anything to be true, it must be tangible. In other words, it must be able to be weighed and measured. This theory forms the foundation of the philosophy of the physical sciences.)

But theology, not the empirical method, is the way to worship our God, who is over mind and matter. And thus theology is the 'queen of all sciences', as it was known in the universities of the Middle Ages. For what is greater to think about, to investigate and to seek to define and understand more precisely, than God Himself? It is the chief end of the whole universe to engage with God and understand Him more deeply. Jesus encourages us to love the Lord God with all our heart, soul and mind (Matthew 22:37). To worship God for ever must involve the use of our minds and our understanding, so that we know better who it is that we glorify. And so theology is the most important of all disciplines and sciences. In this book, therefore, we will engage deeply with the doctrine of the Trinity and find its unique, wonderful and thoroughly worship-evoking contribution to making sense of the universe.

## Why should we study the Trinity?

We need the Trinity to make sense of a complex and interdependent universe. Attempts to find a rationale for why there is such a diversity in our universe have led in some cultures to polytheism (belief in many gods). On the other hand, the unity we find in the universe has suggested to others either a non-personal god, or life force, that is found in everything (monism, sometimes called 'pantheism'), or a monotheistic deity – a god living in his own solitariness, whose personality is really redundant as there is no one to be 'personal' with (until he creates someone). However, a Trinitarian God, being a diversity *within* a unity, makes sense of a universe that also has a diversity within a unity: the creation reflects the Creator, and, what is more, He is full of personal relationship and has never been alone. We will return to look in more depth at all of these ideas.

It is inevitable then that if we hope to get into the depths of the God who made this universe, we will touch some profundities. I hope that this book will bring some part of these truths to you in such a way that you become excited about them and want to know more.

Some people seem to think that the Trinity is such an irrational or impenetrable mystery that it can have no real impact on the Christian life. This is far from being the case, and so, to complete this introduction, I want to set down briefly five reasons (out of many possible ones) why we should study the Trinity. The Trinity is in fact a very important, reasonable and rational concept, forming the basis of many fundamental principles and touching many practical areas of our walk with the Lord. I shall develop these five reasons later in the book: church unity, which leads to world evangelization; the pre-eminence of love; the need to defend Trinitarianism against opponents; practical implications of a Trinitarian theology, and finally, its fundamental implications on church life.

## 1. Church unity for world evangelization

The way in which we understand the Trinity is, in fact, closely linked to our understanding of church unity. The unity of the

Church and the concept of the Trinity are so closely bound together that church history has gone through various phases of unity as our understanding of the Trinity has deepened. At times, church unity has clearly centred upon the person of Christ as, for example, from the time of the Reformation in the sixteenth century until the nineteenth century. At other times the Church has experienced a unity that we might call a 'unity of the Spirit', as with the charismatic movements in the twentieth century.

But I believe there is a unity that is not only the *unity of the Spirit in the bond of peace* (Ephesians 4:3), and that is not only that we are *all one in Christ Jesus* (Galatians 3:28). There is also a unity that comes about through the Father and engages us as sons and daughters in the Trinitarian family of Father, Son and Spirit. We can see this unity of the Father as Jesus prays for His disciples:

> . . . that they may all be one; even as you, Father, are in Me and I in you, that they also may be in Us, so that the world may believe that You sent Me. (John 17:21)

This is the true ecumenism that will form the Church into one body. This prayer shows how the Trinity lies at the heart of a restored expression of unity. It also shows how this unity will bring about the completion of world evangelization. If we, the Church, ignore the doctrine of the Trinity and the unity that it brings, we will certainly hinder the fulfilment of God's purpose that, through His people, *all the nations of the earth might be blessed* (see Genesis 12:3; 18:18).

## 2. *The pre-eminence of love*
I find it strange that, of all the official creeds of the Church – including the Apostles' Creed (which began to be formulated in the third century), the Nicene Creed in the fourth century, the

official creeds of Protestantism in the sixteenth to the nineteenth centuries, the Westminster Confession in the seventeenth century, and even the Evangelical Alliance's doctrinal basis of faith in the nineteenth and twentieth centuries – not one asserts that God is love (1 John 4:16). This verse in John's epistle is a unique Christian assertion, and we should be proud of it, boast of it and declare it – and, of course, live it!

If God in His essential being and person is love, He must have someone to bestow His love upon. You cannot love without an object – except for self-love, which is not really love at all, and especially not as defined for us in the Bible. So, when there was only God, before He created the universe and all the beings within it, how could He be loving? The answer is found in the Trinity! God is three persons in one beautiful relationship of love – the Father loving the Son, the Son loving the Spirit, the Spirit loving the Father, and so on, in an eternal, dynamic expression of love.

The pre-eminence of love depends upon the concept of a plurality or, more specifically, a Trinity within God. For if God were singular, love would not be eternal but would have a beginning only when God created something to love (ie, the universe). If that were the case, love would not be pre-eminently above all else. However, we believe it *is* pre-eminent, and its absoluteness is our safeguard against lesser values being made absolutes – absolutes that then become gods, for which their devotees will even kill. It is for this reason that the German Marxist Kautsky said that he feared anyone who had an absolute in his life. However, the Christian absolute of love does not destroy, but gives life.

## 3. *Defending Trinitarianism against opponents*
Throughout the history of the Church there have been opponents to the doctrine of the Trinity. If, therefore, we are going to be

able to give a reason *for the hope that lies within us* (1 Peter 3:15), we are going to have to look into the doctrine for ourselves and understand why we believe what we believe.

For example, the Ebionites in the first century attacked the Trinity on the basis of their belief that Jesus was not divine and therefore could not be part of the Godhead.

The Arians in the fourth century held that Christ was a created being, perhaps heavenly or angelic, but still not part of the Godhead.

Then there are the modern-day opponents. For example, if you are debating with a Muslim today, the first objection they are likely to present to you is that Christianity is not a reasonable religion because we believe that three can be one. The Trinity is therefore incredible, they would say, because it is philosophically unsound. The Jehovah's Witnesses maintain that Jesus was not God and also support a deistic, or Unitarian, approach.

Even in the newer church scene, there is a branch of Pentecostalism (largely in the United States) that baptizes only in the name of Jesus, thereby denying the necessity of the Trinity as three distinct persons. They believe that the Son, the Father and the Spirit are all just different aspects of the same person: Jesus.

Many liberal theologians also wonder why Christians need to bother defending the Trinity. They would hold that it is a doctrine born out of Greek philosophy and later imposed upon the simple truths of Jesus. 'Isn't it enough,' they would argue, 'simply to love our neighbour and turn the other cheek? Why make ourselves vulnerable by getting tied up in fanciful speculations about the nature of God?'

We need to think these kinds of arguments through seriously and try to understand what the Bible is seeking to teach and why. We will look at these arguments in more detail in chapter six.

## 4. Practical implications

Understanding the doctrine of the Trinity is not just a pursuit for academics and theologians to while away the time in their ivory towers. It has many very practical implications for the Christian life and for the way in which we are Church together. For example, if God is a Trinity, then how should we worship Him? Do we address the Father, Jesus or the Spirit in our prayers, or can we pray to all three? If God is a Trinity, He must be relational, so how does that influence my relationship with Him and with other believers? These are just three of the implications of getting to grips with the Trinity!

## 5. Fundamental implications for church life

Finally, the Trinity in being and existence is fundamental for church life. John Zizioulas, the Metropolitan of Pergamon, in his book *Being as Communion* states that the Church is not simply an institution, but a mode of existence or 'way of being', and then goes on to explain that this is because the God whom the Church is called to reveal to the world also exists in the same way.

This is God's way of existence – as relationship or way of being. The challenge to us to live true church life is to aspire to live in the mode of God's existence, which is fellowship, communion and relationship. Now these are ours – the Church's. Jesus prays that we should share this kind of life both now and in eternity:

> This is eternal life, that they may know You, the only true
> God, and Jesus Christ whom You have sent. (John 17:3)

To show this life of God with God and with each other seems to be our ultimate end and highest aspiration. For this reason, taking communion in this age brings us to the true heart of church life, because we are sharing with one another the way that God exists.

## Analogy

Lastly, before we begin our study proper, I want to say a word or two about analogy. It is almost impossible to talk about the Trinity without referring to analogies and figures, models and symbolism – and this can sometimes make people feel uneasy about being misled into a so-called 'fantastical' realm, rather than the 'truth'. However, the fact that we have to talk about God in analogies or metaphors should be no surprise to us: the Bible is full of imagery intended to help us to understand God better – light, wind, fire, lions, eagles, and so on. Equally, our everyday lives are full of analogies that enable us to talk about things we cannot see. For example, when we say that a 'current' of electricity is 'running through' a wire, we are using an analogy – rivers have currents, not electricity. We need this analogy, or model, as we don't really know what electricity is, but if we think of it like a river we can make sense of how it behaves. Again, we say that subatomic particles are used to 'bombard' atoms, and scientists use analogies such as billiard balls bouncing off one another. This is not, of course, what is really happening: things aren't literally 'bouncing off' one another – in fact no one fully understands what is actually happening in quantum physics – but the analogy is useful. It helps us to picture what is happening and to talk about it in a way that is a *reflection* of what is really going on. Much of life is a great mystery that can only be understood through metaphors that give some form or expression to a particular truth.

There is, in fact, a strict sense in which language itself is metaphorical. The noises I make when I am speaking are merely vacuous entities in and of themselves; they don't really convey anything at all unless the listener engages his or her mind and forms images that correspond to the images I have in my mind. Words are vehicles which hold an idea and convey it from one mind to another. Although analogical language may well be limited, inadequate or imprecise, that does not invalidate it. We have to use analogies to talk about things: they give us an opportunity to get a grip on something intangible and then start to use it. While we may well find ourselves struggling with some words for God, we still have to use words to capture and communicate what we are talking about – whether in science, theology, art or, in fact, anything.

Some people don't like to talk about God as being *three persons*. It is important to remember that we are using an analogy here: when the Early Church used the word 'person' to refer to the members of the Godhead, it had a slightly different meaning to the way in which we use the word today. Thus, some have argued that God has only one will, that the Father, Son and Holy Spirit operate as 'One Will' and therefore as one 'person'. But Jesus said, 'Father, *Your will* be done, not *Mine!*' The Father has a will, the Son has a will, and the Holy Spirit gives gifts according to *His* will (1 Corinthians 12:11). We have to start with the biblical revelation and then build on that. The experience of *willing* something must be at least part of what it means to be a 'person'. Therefore, it must be acceptable to talk about the 'three persons of the Trinity' even though we are using analogical and metaphorical language.

There will be times, as we discuss the Trinity, when we will get caught between different models, when different analogies of three in one (eg, spirit/mind/body, or emotions/mind/will) will not entirely fit together. No picture is totally adequate. So it is not surprising if some of our models of God at times leave us a little puzzled.

Now we are ready to start our study. We will begin by spending some time in exegesis, that is, looking at the Scriptures and the different biblical pictures, and trying to put them together to give us a coherent understanding of the Trinity.

# 1

# Windows into the Trinity

In this chapter we are going to look at three 'windows' that afford us a view of the Trinity. These windows will helps us to get a grasp on the subject and will give us a starting point for further analysis. These are the Scriptural window, the Philosophical window and the Experiential window.

## The Scriptural window

In the Old Testament, the Jews worshipped *Yahweh* as the one true God:

> The LORD is our God, the LORD is one!
> (Deuteronomy 6:4)

Yet in the New Testament we are introduced to Jesus, who is repeatedly referred to as 'Lord', and we are encouraged to believe that He, too, is God. Thomas worshipped Him as such:

> My Lord and my God! (John 20:28)

How do we put it all together? Despite the efforts of post-modernism to the contrary, no rational human mind can really hold overt contradictions together at the same time. Yet we all have to deal with apparent contradictions or paradoxes, particularly with one another in our human relationships. Even the best of lovers have to work at it – in relationship we are trying to integrate our ideas about someone into a comprehensive picture. This is how the human mind is, and so it is when it comes to this doctrine. We have to look carefully at the Scriptures to see how they offer us the means to understand what may otherwise, at face value, appear as a contradiction.

## The Old Testament

Although some people have dismissed this interpretation, I think there are four clear places in the Old Testament where the concept of plurality within the Godhead is presented. We shall look at these four passages first, before moving on to other passages in the Old Testament.

These four passages indicate a plurality in a singularity – not necessarily the Trinity, to begin with, but at least more than two persons in the Godhead. Hebrew has a singular and a plural, like English. But, unlike English, it has also a *dual*, to refer to 'two' people or things. The four passages we are about to look at use the plural, not the dual, which therefore means they are referring to three, at the least.

## Plurality within the Godhead
• Genesis 1:26–27

> Then God said, 'Let Us make man in Our image, according to Our likeness; and let them rule over the fish of the sea and over the birds of the sky and over the cattle and over all the earth, and over every creeping thing that creeps on the earth.' God created man in His own image, in the image of God, He created him; male and female He created them.

These verses are a lovely sort of mix-up, back and forth! They begin with God saying 'let *Us*'. Those who do not like the idea of a hint at a Trinity or some plurality within the Godhead will say, 'God must have been speaking to the angels'. But why should God say 'let Us make man in Our image' to the angels? He would be saying that the angels also bear His image and that humankind was being made like them. But it is only to His creature, humankind, that the defining word of God is given that they would be in God's image (v27). We never read in the Bible that God said these words to heavenly creatures such as angels.

Some might try to avoid the concept of a plurality in a singularity by saying that God was speaking with 'the plural of majesty' – like Queen Victoria's famous saying '*We* are not amused' when referring to herself. I don't think that we should interpret the Bible simply on the grounds of Queen Victoria's lack of a sense of humour! But the Hebrews did express themselves like that. They sometimes used a plural to intensify a statement. However, if we look at the verse again, it goes on to say:

> 'Let Us make man in *Our* image, according to *Our* likeness' . . . and God created man in *His* own image.

'*Our* image' changes to '*His* own image'. The simplest and most reasonable deduction is that the 'Us' is a 'Him'. This immediately brings the idea of a plurality into a concept of singularity. More than that, having said 'let Us make *man* in Our image', the Scripture immediately says '. . . male and female, He created *them*'. His creatures, human beings, exist in a plurality, male and female, and so we are being driven to consider that maybe just as humankind can only be originally understood in terms of plurality – 'male and female' – so even God himself can only be understood fully as a plurality. The definition of humankind as 'male' means nothing unless there is the 'female'. There has to be a female to correspond with the male. So already we are getting a hint that, within the Godhead, the idea of 'God' might well necessitate at least one other counterpart or component.

• Genesis 3:22

> Then the LORD God said, 'Behold, the man has become like one of *Us*, knowing good and evil; and now, he might stretch out his hand and take also from the tree of life and eat, and live forever.'

Here, once again, we find God speaking as an 'Us'.

• Genesis 11:7

> 'Come, let *Us* go down and there confuse their language . . .'

This verse also raises the question: is this the 'plural of majesty', or does it indicate that within God there are counsels that take place between the Father, Son and Holy Spirit?

• Isaiah 6:8

> Then I heard the voice of the Lord saying, 'Whom shall *I* send, and who will go for *Us*?'

This is perhaps the most famous occurrence of a plurality juxtaposed with a singularity in reference to God in the Old Testament.

In all of the passages above we see that, indeed, the Old Testament contains this concept of a God who is both singular and plural – even in its first chapters. It is true that God was known as 'one' in the pre-patriarchal times (and on into patriarchal times). And this is no surprise, as nearly every culture in antiquity and every primitive religion held to the concept of a 'one Creator god' who was to be approached by means of sacrifice.

One example of this primeval revelation being retained in ancient myths is the Greek story of Achilles' heel, which is clearly the ancient revelation of Genesis 3:15 '. . . you shall bruise him on the heel', twisted and now a legend of Greek mythology. (Another is found in Genesis 6, where the offspring of divine and human encounters produced giants, or great heroes, among which we could imagine Hercules, who was the product of a god going 'in to the daughters of men'. Also, the flood story is found in many cultures of the ancient world, but in fantastical forms.)

The roots of this ancient revelation of God to us are planted in God's first declaration of the gospel – the serpent's head will be crushed, but the heel of the seed that would come to crush him would be bitten. Some of the ancient revelation of God still existed in the cultures of humankind in this mythologized form. But by the time Abraham was in Ur of the Chaldees (C. 2000 BC), the occult priest-craft of the Babylonians had spread throughout the human race, perverting and confusing the revelation of this Creator God into the worship of many gods (polytheism). It was therefore God's purposeful counter-attack to choose Abraham and begin to purify the ancient revelations that had been given to humanity. Abraham's task was to teach his children from God's true revelation so that ultimately, through his later descendants, Israel, the ancient revelation would be rescued and purged of such accretions. The world could one day come back to the *one* God, the Creator, the One approached by sacrifice, from whom further revelations concerning our future hope would be filtered into humankind's history. In Abraham, God says:

All the nations of the earth will be blessed. For I have
known him, so that he may command his children . . .
to keep the way of the LORD. (Genesis 18:18–9)

(For more on God's plan for humanity, see my and Paul Marston's
book *God's Strategy in Human History, Volume 1: God's Path to
Victory.*)

*The oneness of God*
It is in this context of confusing and deceptive polytheism that
monotheism, the uniqueness and the sole Oneness of God, is
largely presented and emphasized by the patriarchs in the Old
Testament. But, even within this picture of monotheism that is
painted, we still find hints at a plurality.

• Deuteronomy 6:4
The great Shema speech (Hebrew *shema* means 'to hear') tells us:

Hear, O Israel! The LORD is our God, the LORD is one!

The Hebrew word for 'one' here is *echad*. This is the same word for
'one' which is used in Genesis 2:24 '. . . and the two shall become
*one* flesh'. *Yachiyd*, on the other hand, means sole, exclusive,
complete entity in itself; uniqueness. The word *yachiyd* is used to
describe Abraham offering his 'unique', his beloved 'one and only'
son (Genesis 22:2, 12, 16; see also Zechariah 12:10). But God
does not use *yachiyd* of Himself here. Instead He uses *echad*, which
can speak of two in one flesh, a plurality within a singularity. Even
in the midst of promoting unique monotheism in a world of
polytheism, God uses a word that has a further revelation within
it of plurality. There might be something like the 'one flesh-ness'
of human marriage in the one being of God Himself.

• Isaiah 48:16–49:1

The following Old Testament statement can be understood clearly
in Trinitarian terms:

> Come near to Me, listen to this: From the first I have
> not spoken in secret. From the time it took place, I
> was there. And now the Lord God has sent Me and
> His Spirit.

Somebody is speaking and saying that the *Lord God* has sent *Him*
and *His Spirit*. If we move down a few verses to 'Listen to *Me*, O
islands . . .' (49:1), presumably we meet the same 'Me' addressing
the situation. And that 'Me' goes on to say:

> The LORD called Me from the womb. From the body
> of My mother, He named Me.

This is a wonderful prophecy of the coming Messiah whose name,
'Jesus', was not revealed in the Old Testament because these verses
tell us it would not be mentioned until He was in His mother's
womb. The 'Me' who is talking here is the Messiah, who has
been sent by the Lord God – as indeed the Spirit has been, too
('the Lord God has sent Me, and His Spirit'). Here is a beautiful
preparation for further revelation of the Trinitarian God, coming
out of the Old Testament text.

## The New Testament

• Matthew

The Old Testament is concerned to hone down our view of God to
monotheism, while leaving seeds of some deeper plurality, which
now the New Testament begins to take up. Artlessly, and without
any explanation, Jesus speaks about God in such terms that you
would not think He was claiming divinity. But, then in the next

breath, He speaks with divine authority and expects (and accepts) all honour, and it is accrued to Jesus Himself, as God. He is worshipped, and He takes all the prerogatives of God. Jesus said:

> You have heard that the ancients were told [by God] 'You shall not commit murder' . . . but *I* say to you that everyone who is angry with his brother shall be liable before the court. (Matthew 5:21–2)

Thus He promotes Himself, though always in the humble-hearted way of the Messiah, as His words reinterpret God's Old Testament law. Again Jesus said, 'He who loves father or mother more than Me is not worthy of Me' – and says the same also of our children and our lives (Matthew 10:37–9). Who can make such claims, that He should be loved beyond parents, wife, children or anyone else? Only God! Jesus was either absolutely arrogant, or deranged in His mind, or else making a claim to be God.

So the New Testament presents us with a duality within the Godhead: Father and Son. And, just as we are trying to get our heads around that, it gets more complicated!

• John 14:16, 26
Jesus said:

> I will ask the Father, and He will send you another Helper . . . whom the Father will send in My name . . .

At Pentecost a new era began. The Spirit could be spoken to personally (presumably so, if He is to teach, guide, disclose and listen – see for example John 14:26, Acts 16:6–10, John 16:13–5). If the Spirit was around, then God was around (Acts 11:15–8). We find a New Testament revelation of God as three: Father, Son and Spirit. Jesus also promises that the Father and the Spirit, as well as He Himself, will set up their abode in us (John 14:16–23).

We need not feel uneasy about our threefold God. We shall see later that even Islam, which seeks to assert itself as the defender of purist monotheism, is driven to accept three eternals: Allah, the eternal Koran and the eternal spirit of Allah. This seems suspiciously close to our own Trinity! How is this the case? It is because we cannot think adequately about this complex universe in which we live without ultimately being driven towards the necessity of a Trinity being at the base of it.

• Matthew 28:16–9

> . . . the eleven disciples proceeded to Galilee, to the mountain which Jesus had designated. When they saw Him, they worshipped; but some were doubtful. (v16-7)

These monotheistic Jews are worshipping Jesus. They are forbidden to worship anyone other than God, and yet they worship Jesus. Verses 18–19 say:

> And Jesus came up and spoke to them, saying, 'All authority has been given to Me in heaven and on earth. Go therefore and make disciples of all the nations, baptizing them in the Name of the Father and the Son and the Holy Spirit.'

It is interesting to note that the word 'Name' is in the singular in the Greek text, but the name is of the Father, Son and Holy Spirit. Is there one name for Father, Son and Holy Spirit together? As we have said, some believe that the one name is Jesus and so they baptize in the name of Jesus only. Some have said that the one name is God. But 'God' is not quite a name – it's more of a designation. Rather, 'Lord' is the name that is above every name. Every knee shall bow and every tongue confess that Jesus is Lord. The name 'Lord' is most probably to be understood in terms of the Father, Son and Holy Spirit, since 'Lord' refers to both Jesus and the Father in the Bible very frequently, and even the Spirit is called 'Lord' in 2 Corinthians 3:18. Perhaps 'Lord' is the one name for the three-in-one God. The Old Testament bears this out by using *Elohiym*, a plural for the word 'Lord'.

• 1 Corinthians 8:4–6

The Apostle Paul, in the epistle of 1 Corinthians, expands the great Hebrew credal 'Shema' statement found in Deuteronomy 6:4 that we looked at above.

Hear, O Israel! The LORD is our God, the LORD is one!

Paul takes this monotheistic Scripture and unravels, or perhaps better *unpeels,* the diversity found in one God.

The instruction Paul is giving is in relation to how Chrisitians are to interact with non-Christians when it comes to eating together when the feast has been offered to idols. Is a Christian compromised if they knowingly or inadvertently eat a meal which contains meat that has been sacrificed to idols?

'There are many gods and many lords', says Paul (earlier in verse 5 qualifying these gods as 'so-called'). '. . . yet for us there is but one God, the Father . . . and one Lord . . .' Now, in the Old Testament context both 'God' and 'the Lord' are clearly the same being. The word 'Lord' is really *Yahweh*, the name God gave Moses at the burning bush (Exodus 3:14) – a name so sacred that the Jews never uttered it, but put into it the vowels from *Adonai* (that is 'Lord') to produce the name *Jehovah*! But Paul now separates the two: God and Lord. The *one* God is

the Father, from whom are all things and we exist for Him . . . (v6)

Paul then takes the second word 'Lord' and the word 'one', which in Deuteronomy 6:4 belongs to both God and Lord, and adds:

> . . . and *one* Lord, Jesus Christ, by whom are all things, and we exist through Him.

And there is more, for the God who is the Lord also has the anointing ('Christ' means *anointed one*), that is, the Holy Spirit. The Hebrew monotheistic God is also the Lord and the anointing. Paul has peeled off the layers of the Trinity and we are gazing at Jesus, who shows us the depths of God by the Spirit who dwells in us.


• 1 Thessalonians 1:1 *&* 2 Thessalonians 1:1–2
Paul also picks up on the 'Shema' statement of Deuteronomy 6:4 in the first verses of both Thessalonian epistles.

As we can see from many of the verses we look at in this section, Paul, amongst other New Testament writers, alluded quite freely to two persons of the Godhead without any explanation or embarrassment. He obviously assumed his converts would understand his assertions. The first verses of 1 and 2 Thessalonians are of particular significance, because these epistles are the earliest New Testament writings, dating from 50AD.

> Paul and Silvanus and Timothy, to the church of the Thessalonians in God the Father and the Lord Jesus Christ: Grace to you and peace. (1 Thessalonians 1:1)

> Paul and Silvanus and Timothy, to the church of the Thessalonians in God our Father and the Lord Jesus Christ: Grace to you and peace from God the Father and the Lord Jesus Christ. (2 Thessalonians 1:1–2)

Here Paul takes the first title of the Shema, 'God', and applies it to the Father, and takes the second title, 'Lord' (*Yahweh* or *Jehovah*), and applies it to the Son, Jesus. However, Paul keeps the two titles close together by governing both with the same preposition in each case. In so doing he shows they are together the source of the Church and of grace.

In the light of this earliest known Christian use of God and Lord from the Jewish creedal statement, it seems completely out of the question to assert, as many critics have, that Jesus was only elevated into the status of a deity in the fourth and fifth centuries at the councils of Nicea and Chalcedon as a product of evolving legend. These occurrences in writings from just 27 years after Jesus' crucifixion and resurrection show that from the very beginning of the Christian era Jesus was regarded on a par with God the Father, and co-functioning with Him. The word 'Trinity' was coined in the second century as a shorthand way of writing this conviction when the deity of the Spirit (ie anointing or Christ-ing) of God was also included in the statements of God's being and activites.

• 1 Corinthians 12:3–6
Here Paul talks about the gifts of the Holy Spirit and how we function in those gifts.

> Therefore I make known to you, that no one speaking by the Spirit of God says, 'Jesus is accursed'; and no one can say, 'Jesus is Lord,' except by the Holy Spirit. Now there are varieties of gifts, but the same Spirit. And there are varieties of ministries, and the same Lord. There are varieties of effects, but the same God who works all things in all persons.

In talking about the gifts and their use, in explaining how we should engage in various ministries and allow the energizing and the working of God in our lives, Paul confronts us with a Trinitarian formula. We need to know something about God (the Father), something about the Son, the Lord and something about the Spirit if we are to have the gifts operating fully in our lives. Perhaps the reason we get into so much trouble with the actual operation of the gifts, or do not see them at work at all, is because we are not Trinitarian in our approach to the manifestation of the Spirit. We need to understand God in a Trinitarian way in order to have a comprehensive and balanced experience of Christian ministry and the operation of our gifts.

• 2 Corinthians 13:14
Paul blesses the Corinthians by saying:

> The grace of our Lord Jesus Christ, and the love of God, and the fellowship of the Holy Spirit, be with you all.

This is an alternative New Testament blessing parallel to the blessing given by the high priest when he came before Israel and said 'Lord' three times:

> The LORD bless you and keep you, the LORD make His face shine on you and be gracious to you, the LORD lift up His countenance on you and give you peace.
> (Numbers 6:24–6)

It is interesting that the priestly blessing was threefold, and Paul uses the three persons of the Trinity to mirror that blessing as he reinterprets it in the New Testament. Paul built on the Old Testament threefold revelation to help us understand clearly what the Israelites could only grasp intuitively: that the God we worship can only adequately be spoken about in threefold terms. There are many other places, not only in Paul's letters, where this kind of allusion to a Trinitarian formula appears, for example, Romans 8:8–11, Galatians 4:6, Ephesians 2:19–22 and 3:14–7, 1 Thessalonians 5:18–9, 2 Thessalonians 2:13–4, 1 Peter 1:2 and 4:14 and 1 John 4:10–6.

• Revelation 22:13–19

In the final chapter of the Bible, Revelation 22, the three persons of the Trinity are clearly visible – Jesus (v16), The Spirit (v17) and God the Father (v18–9).

Just before that, in verse 13 Jesus says:

> I am the Alpha and the Omega, the first and the last, the beginning and the end. (see also Revelation 1:8, 21:6)

Here Jesus is defined as 'the beginning' (compare also John 1:1–3), and this takes us right the way back to the start of the Bible in Genesis 1:1–2, where we can now see the Trinity beginning to emerge:

> In *the beginning* God created the heavens and the earth. The earth was formless and void, and darkness was over the surface of the deep, and the Spirit of God was moving over the surface of the waters.

So God the Father created the heavens and the earth in the beginning, ie *in Jesus*. The universe came into being through Jesus, *the* Beginning. Not only that but in Genesis 1 we also see the Holy Spirit – the 'Spirit of God' – bringing form and life.

So the Trinity appears together in the first two verses of the Bible and in the last few verses, like bookends that hold the whole book together from Genesis to Revelation, demonstrating that Jesus is indeed the beginning and the end, not only of creation and all things, but also of Scripture.

## The Philosophical window

We have seen the Trinity through the window of Scripture and theological reasoning. Let us turn now to philosophy, to look at whether there is a rational as well as a theological case in our favour. I have hinted already at the philosophical necessity to have some sort of distinction and diversity within the Godhead because of the complexity of our universe. Let us now consider a key question of philosophy: how do we know that we exist? The thought that something cannot exist in isolation might be novel or unusual for most of us, as we have obviously never been in a complete void. Even as our mother's fertilized egg begins to divide to form us, her heartbeat is there to show that we are not alone. Let me try to unpack this problem of existence a bit more.

Try to imagine a god who is not a Trinitarian god, existing in an eternity of nothingness. Our concept of being, or existence, requires that we relate to something else – otherwise we have no way of knowing that we are there. Consequently, could such a god be aware of his own self if he had nothing from which to distinguish himself, no way of saying, 'this is me; this is not me'? His being, and consequently his sense of self, would be indistinguishable from nothingness. In short, he would not exist. One might reply, with Descartes, 'I think, therefore I am.' This phrase has been cited as the cornerstone of rationalism and seems to fly in the face of what we are discussing. Descartes' sentence, however, is seldom completed: 'I think, therefore I am and God is.' Descartes knew that, among other things, we cannot exist as individuals in a void. Now, when we have tried to think of a single-unit, sole-entity god who exists within a vast, blank eternity, that god is meaningless. He cannot know he is there, because he has nothing to relate to. He does not know who he is or even why he exists. It is this conclusion that drives us philosophically to think that God must be sufficient within himself. But if he were a God who could relate to someone else within himself, then he could be self-sufficient.

The Trinitarian God is one who can meet these requirements. The Father relates to the Son, the Son to the Spirit and the Spirit to the Father, and so on. And it is within that counsel or party, within that interaction of the three persons of the Trinity, that God can define Himself, know who He is and be aware that He exists. The Christian God is utterly sufficient in Himself; He is conscious of Himself; He knows Himself; He is able to integrate within Himself and therefore can be a Creator who relates to His creation. We need a Trinitarian God; we simply cannot do without one – philosophically, theologically, emotionally or experientially. I hope that this relationship within the Trinitarian God begins to excite you.

Now, since we exist, we presumably have been created. The argument that God has to exist in order for anything to be created, because something cannot be created from nothing unless there is a separate and discrete creative agent, is known as the cosmological argument. If, therefore, there is a Creator, he would have to be the sort of Creator who existed, and knew he existed, before he made us. This means that the cosmological argument for the existence of God must be a Trinitarian one, according to what we have just considered – that only such a God would know of his own existence and therefore conceive of a plan to create.

So, then, why are there monists and pluralists? Monism is the view that *all* things are one with a single moral force, or god. Monists hold their view because they see that we live in a *uni*verse where *everything* holds and belongs together in, of and to itself. While it is true that our God is the source and Creator of all, monism fails because it doesn't explain the diversity, the chaos and the conflict that is evident in our universe. Our universe is a *uni-verse*. Yes, it is 'uni' (singular), but the 'verse' has within its Latin roots the idea of sequential, connected and disconnected things, turnings and opposites. It is not just a One: the universe is diverse. It is not a bland, unresponsive, predetermined and unchanging thing held together by an impersonal, monistic glue, which hardly deserves the name 'god'.

Standing against the monists, then, are pluralists. They see the great variety and distinctions within this universe and, not least, they see themselves as distinct from everybody else. In this context of variety, the polytheists (those who believe specifically in many gods) come into the picture. Their explanation is that there is a pantheon of gods who spend their time in eternal conflict, jockeying for position. They see the need for a god of war, a god of peace, a god of sex, and so on, to explain the multifaceted nature of our life. Polytheism looks like a great chaos; everything is fighting against everything else, and the outcome of any interactions in the spiritual, moral, social or physical world is arbitrary or based on the relative powers of the gods. Polytheism doesn't explain the underlying order, the structure or the cohesion of our world.

The God we worship is neither monistic nor polytheistic. A God who embraces both emphases, He is the only philosophically adequate God that can exist within this universe. We have also demonstrated that, in order to know himself, a monotheistic god has to be at least a duality, if not a Trinity, or potentially even more! Just think of the terrific advantage we should have as Christians when it comes to answering Hinduism with both its monism and polytheism, and Islam with its inadequate and impossible monotheism. These are the two biggest alternative religions. Here is the Trinity in the tension of the argument, holding the answer for both sides. Our God, as Father, Son and Spirit, brings everything together into one, yet we maintain all the richness and variety of the polytheists (and their freedom and diversity) in our Trinitarian God. Christians should be winning hands down on converts if we worship and love and know this God, because we have the answers in Him. I am not ashamed to say that Jesus is the answer! Where else do I go if I have a question? We have a God who is the source of all answers, because He is the source of everything.

## The Experiential window

Scripturally, we have established that the Trinity is evident from the opening of Genesis; and philosophically, that we cannot understand the nature of God logically without there being a plurality and, in our case, a Trinity. But how does the Trinity impact us experientially? This is a valid question, though not one on which we would place a casting vote without theological or philosophical evidence. We live by faith, and not by sight (which is empiricism) or feeling. We experience God in three fundamental ways.

### Over and above us

We experience God comprehensively as a God who is over and above us, the God of the heavenly dominion. He is no God at all who is not a God of authority, who brings that authority meaningfully into the universe. The authority of a government, the authority of a headteacher, the authority of the police force is meaningless unless there is a God; otherwise, authority is just up for grabs for anyone who is big, strong and bold enough to take over. Earthly authority means nothing unless there is a God who is the embodiment of authority: the Creator who has a purpose for us, whose dominion over us helps us to submit to the authority we exercise over one another where it is in line with His will for the universe. In a theistic system, the meaning for humanity can only come from what God meant us to be. Whenever we have plans for the world, whenever we exert our authority to get something changed in our circumstances, whenever we search for meaning and purpose in our lives, we are touching into the God who is over and above us, bringing order, authority, meaning and purpose into our existence.

*With us and one of us*
We also experience the God who is with us and has gone before us – we follow Him, God the Son, Jesus, Emmanuel, because He is one of us. We can follow Him because He has gone before us. When we are talking about our needs or walking the way of the martyr, we talk to Jesus and ask Him how He lived through it; when we want to know what we should be doing with our lives, we try to follow Jesus. We become aware that we are talking to somebody who can sympathize with us, as the writer to the Hebrews says, because He has been through all these things (4:15). We experience God as someone not just distant and wholly other than us, but as someone who understands us, who is with us, who has been there before us. That is the God of our communion, as we have fellowship with Jesus – 'We love you, Lord Jesus, because You are one of us' (Hermann Hesse, quoted in *The Waiting Father* by Helmut Thielicke, p. 50).

*Within us*
There are times when we experience God as something that is going on within us. God is moving inside. He was the reason we fell on our knees when we prayed, or lifted up holy hands. You may have felt moved from inside as you stood on the top

of a mountain and lifted your hands up – what else could you do? The God in you was reaching out to the God out there. We find that God is in us, leading us and giving us experiences and acting intuitively within us. In the otherwise rational person, that must be God! When our hearts burn within us, or we weep at the intensity of beauty, that is the Spirit of God. The God over and above us has dominion; the God with us and before us is the God that we follow and have communion with; the God within us is the God whom, in one sense, we possess, but who, in another sense, possesses us. The God of dominion, the God of communion and the God of possession – we belong to Him, He owns us, but we also own Him – He is *our* God!

These three experiences of God in life show us three different ways in which God relates to us. As we begin to appreciate them more and more, we become aware that the only way we can talk about this God is in a Trinitarian form. Let's now turn to consider the depth and complexity that the Trinity brings to our understanding of, and relationship with, the Godhead. We will begin with some more theology, for this always has to be our starting point: God's revelation of Himself through what He has given us in Scripture. In the following chapters we will examine the characteristics of our triune God from various angles, beginning with a critique of some of the Greek influences on Western theology.

# 2

# A Moved, Moving Mover

We know nothing about God unless He reveals himself to us – that is logical. But that does not mean that we can invent what He is like: it means that we are dependent on Him telling us. Revelation is a logical necessity if we are ever going to know anything about God, just as it is a logical necessity that if I am to know *you*, you must reveal yourself to me through your words and actions.

## The effect of Aristotelian thought

Aristotle said that God is '*the unmoved mover*' – the first cause of everything in the universe – as if God was the cue that began the cosmic billiards game by sending the white ball into the reds to disperse them in their different directions. He started off moving by himself, moved everything else and then he stopped moving, stopped being involved, and just left his universe to play out the repercussions of his action on its own. Thus he is the 'unmoved mover'. I want to disagree with this description. The danger of starting with someone else's definition of God that we have not tried and tested personally, is that when our experience doesn't fit with it, then we are at risk of thinking we have lost God. A lot of people have had this sad experience, and it can be devastating to their faith – but their problem is that they started with a false assumption about God in the first place.

Many colleges begin their courses in theology by giving definitions of God that come from such Greek philosophical assumptions as 'God is the unmoved mover'; 'God is the first cause'; 'God is impassible'; 'God is perfect and therefore cannot change' (that is, 'immutable'). It is with these Greek, and not Hebrew, premises that students are then told to turn to the Bible and search for verses that fit this preconceived doctrine of God. Generally speaking, that is the way that we are taught theology – we go to the Bible to try and find and defend our Greek concept of deity, rather than seeking God's view of Himself. We shall return to this matter of Aristotle's influence later in the chapter.

Most people have a preconceived idea of God that must have come from somewhere and, more often than not, it is from the ancient Greeks! (This is because ancient Greek civilization is considered to be the birthplace of Western thought and culture in its broadest sense. Socrates, Plato, Aristotle, Archimedes, Pythagoras and others have formed the foundation of Western reasoning, mathematics, democratic politics and belief, both through their own writings and through their influence on the Romans. It is not surprising, therefore, that after the apostolic age Greek premises had a major influence on the earliest theologians such as Augustine, who embraced them. For more on the impact of Augustinian theology on Church history, please see my and Paul Marston's book *God's Strategy in Human History, Volume 2: Reconsidering Key Biblical Ideas*.)

When people say, 'I just can't believe that Jesus is God!' you should ask, 'Oh really? You know God, then? What is He like?' How do we know what God is like, to be able to say whether Jesus is God or not? We know absolutely nothing about God until He tells us what He is like. In the same way, you know absolutely nothing about me until I tell you or show you something. I let you know what I like, what I dislike, what I think, what I admire, what I detest, and so on. In the same way, we are dependent upon God's revelation of Himself to us, to know what He is like.

> God, after He spoke long ago to the fathers in the prophets in many portions and in many ways, in these last days has spoken to us in His Son. (Hebrews 1:1–2)

The Old Testament shows us bits and pieces about God, but it is when we come to Jesus that we hear, 'He who has seen Me has seen the Father' (John 14:9). Then we can begin to accept the possibility that God could appear as Jesus, washing His creation's feet and hanging on the cross saying, 'Father, forgive.' When we look at Jesus and we are told that He is the fullness of the Godhead bodily (Colossians 2:9), we know that it is not possible to get any deeper, or more accurately, into the heart of God than that. If that is what God is like, we want to worship Him. We are not trying to prove that Jesus is God. On the contrary, we declare that Jesus reveals God to us and that without Him we know nothing and can know nothing about God. Neither can we imagine what could 'out-God' Him, or out-love Him – He is the best.

Although philosophy is a useful vehicle for communicating truth, it is a bad teacher when it comes to theology. Throughout the academic theological world, and now filtering down into the Church too, people are beginning to recognize that Greek philosophy has imposed itself upon Christian theology in some unhelpful ways, and that it therefore has to be peeled off. We are getting back to the Hebrew basics. Studying Greek is important, not least because God gave us the New Testament revelation in Greek, but it is a Hebrew God that we worship! We worship the

God of Abraham, Isaac and Jacob. So let's start to peel off some of those Greek layers.

*First layer: the existential 'I Am'*
When God introduces himself to Moses as '*Yahweh*', 'I am who I am', in Exodus 3:14, we can take the traditional view through Greek philosophical eyes and say, 'Ah, yes, God is making an existential statement about Himself – "I am the self-existing God, the God who exists in and of Himself, the self-sufficient God, the God who is ultimate being, the God who exists regardless of whether people know Him or acknowledge Him!"'

Well, all of that may be true, but it has nothing to do with what God was saying to Moses when He said 'I am who I am', or, perhaps better, 'I am that I am' or even 'I am am-ing what I am am-ing'! God was trying to communicate. He was not discussing His existential state of being, but rather His evident activity and involvement in the world: *I am the God who your fathers worshipped. I am the God of Abraham, I am the God of Isaac, I am the God of Jacob. I will certainly be with you just as I was with them! I am that I am; I am am-ing it. I am active and at work. That's why you can trust Me when you are before Pharaoh!*

You can see the difference between the self-existent, 'static' God existing out there and the 'am-ing' God down here, who is reassuring Moses, *I will go with you, I will go through the Red Sea with you*. It makes a lot more sense of the story. God affirming His self-sufficient existence would not have been much comfort to Moses as he was about to demand freedom for God's people from Pharaoh's tyranny. It was the dynamic, living God who is with us, active on earth, that Moses needed to encounter – not one who exists in some serene state outside time and space.

*Second layer: the impassible / unmoving God*

Now we come back to the 'unmoved mover' mentioned at the beginning of this chapter. Aristotle's unmoved mover had to be unmoved because the Greeks believed that God, by definition, was perfect. If He was perfect then He could never change, because if He were to change, He would either no longer be perfect, or He would not have been perfect to begin with. A God who cannot change must therefore be *impassible* – that is, unable to feel anything or experience emotion. So God is always the same: He never feels anything, because if He was happy one moment and sad the next He would have changed, and would therefore not be perfect. But how can you have a relationship with a being who feels nothing? You end up trying to relate to a lump of cold marble, which is something like what Aquinas, the great medieval theologian, concluded God must be like, because he accepted Aristotle's definition.

A relationship with the unmoved mover is like wrapping lonely arms round a marble pillar, trying to feel some warmth or comfort but finding only cold, hard impassibility. Some people treat their relationship with God like that. But the God revealed to us in the Bible is one who weeps; the God who is revealed to us in Jesus laughs. Our God is a God who feels and has empathy with us, who comforts us and enters into our experience and builds a relationship with us.

So why do so many think God to be impassible? Because generations of our theologians, and our culture, have accepted this Greek idea of perfection: if you changed, so the argument goes, you could not have been perfect all the time. And so we find a verse for it: 'Jesus Christ, the same yesterday and today and forever' (Hebrews 13:8). That means God doesn't change!

Not at all. Consider changing the premise: suppose one started with the definition that perfection equals the ability to change. You would find another meaning for that verse. There was a time when God was not man and then He became one – He added something to Himself in experiencing humanity. God changed:

> [He] emptied Himself, taking the form of a bond-servant, being made in the likeness of men. (Philippians 2:7)

There was a time when the Spirit was not yet the Spirit of the glorified Man (John 7:39).

The Hebrew God, the dynamic, living God that we deal with, undoubtedly changes, and He is not the philosophical abstraction which we invent for ourselves. Hence, I have re-coined Aristotle's definition of God as the 'unmoved mover' to become the 'moved, moving mover' – a catchy epithet, perhaps. God is 'moved' because He can feel:

- He knows compassion (Psalm 145:8, Hosea 11:8, Isaiah 49:15)
- He is grieved (Genesis 6:6–7)
- He is overwhelmed with anger (Exodus 32:10)
- He is pleasantly surprised (1 Kings 3:10)
- He is unpleasantly surprised (Jeremiah 3:7, 32:35)
- He changes His mind (Exodus 32:14).

He is 'moving' because He is a dynamic, living God. His perfection is that He is always moving and interacting in relationship within Himself. Father, Son and Spirit maintain a dynamic, loving fellowship, a unity in diversity. Finally, God is a 'mover' because it is His life and energy that keeps the universe running. God is alive and doing something with His creation. Creation itself reflects His constant activity: 'in Him all things hold together' (Colossians 1:17). Creation has the Creator's fingerprints all over it for it, and He, are always changing – though His character, of course, remains consistently steadfast and sure.

If you don't change you are dead. God is not dead. Life means movement, and God has created a universe that is full of life and movement, and that should testify that God Himself is alive and moving!

In the next three chapters we are going to look at different models of the Trinity that will help us delve more deeply into the relationships within the Trinity and how they function together.

# 3

# The Song and Dance God

The Early Church soon described the Trinity as a *perichoresis*. This is a transliterated Greek word, probably deriving from *peri*, meaning 'around', and *choreuo*, meaning 'to make room', 'go forward', 'give way' – in other words, meaning 'to dance', or 'dance around'. This word was used in pagan worship when dancing around a particular altar. The Early Church wanted us to see that we worship a song and dance God. When you play three notes together in a chord on the piano you can hear each distinct note, but it all still makes one sound. The different notes work in harmony together. Similarly, there is a harmony that exists within the Godhead. Or you can think of it like a dance, where the partners move around one another, each giving way to the other and then changing the direction, or changing the lead, but each one always in perfect symphony and synchrony. This is the *perichoresis* of the Trinity.

The Cappadocian fathers, whose theology was the most advanced in understanding the Trinity, first used the word *perichoresis* in the fourth century. The music (song) and movement (dance) bind the persons of the Godhead together in a unity, and that is the unified God that we worship. The Latin word for *perichoresis* is *circumcesio*. *Circum* means 'around' and *cesio* probably comes from the verb meaning 'to move in and out' or 'to yield to'. It is very similar to the Greek word in meaning, but you can see the ideas behind the words developing as the Early Church theologians thought about the concept. It is a picture of the Trinity that we have gradually lost over time and replaced with our Aristotelian picture of the static, marble-pillar God who doesn't respond or move at all. But the Greek word *perichoresis* and the Latin word *circumcesio* together build up an image of how these early theologians understood the Trinity. They saw the three persons of the Godhead consistently cohering – that is, holding together in oneness and unison. As they 'danced around' together, they were also 'moving in and out' of one another and thus 'co-inhering', or 'living in', one another.

'Co-inherence' is the more sophisticated way of talking about this dance in which God is involved. The Son lives in the Father, the Father lives in the Son, the Son lives in the Spirit, and so on, so that they are all the time sharing and interacting with each other. They are symbiotically feeding on one another. We could use the analogy of the different organs of a body, which all need each other to share life and move together. This is just another analogy to help us grasp the concept of the relational life that is expressed within the Godhead – the co-inherence, the perichoresis, the God who is ever turning in a holy dance. Father, Son and Spirit, moving in and out of each other's place and position, one moving forward, the other moving backward, each giving place to the other and then taking their own place. That is the movement of a dynamic God who is not an 'unmoved mover'. He is a moving, dancing God who is living in the harmony of heaven, experiencing all the joy and wonder of sharing a dance together. The dance has been developing throughout eternity and has burst forth in the creation of the universe as a glorious expression of joy – which, after all, is what a dance is all about! Harmony and beauty express themselves in this wonderful universe that God has made, and they find their perfect fulfilment as we respond to His invitation to share in the divine dance with Him. So the *pas de trois* God introduces us into becomes a *quadrille* (the Trinity and each one of us makes four), and on into billions of dancers in a dancing universe where hills, skies and valleys of corn clap their hands (Psalm 98:8; Isaiah 55:12) in time to the rhythm of God Himself.

This is the song and dance God. That is the God we read about in the Scriptures. You won't find Him in the ideas that we inherit from Greek philosophy. The God who sings, harmonizes and makes music, 'He will rejoice over you with singing' (Zephaniah 3:17, NIV), who moves and dances and speaks of His procession, or goings, into the sanctuary, in which singers and women with tambourines follow (Psalm 68:24–5, NIV) is the dynamic Hebrew, Trinitarian God. He is not the cold marble pillar of Aristotle and Aquinas; He is the God we need to rediscover if we are going to get to the real heart of Christianity, and the sort of unity that God has given us as His people to reflect who He is. John 14 is a good example of the *perichoresis*. Jesus says in verse 18, 'I will not leave you as orphans; I will come to you', and in verse 28, 'I go away, and I will come to you.' He explains the dynamic in verses 16 and 26: 'I will ask the Father and He will send the Holy Spirit to you in My Name.' And in verse 23, He says, 'The Father and I will come and We will dwell with you.'

Jesus promises that the Father, the Son and the Spirit will dwell within the disciples. Jesus would ask the Father to send the Holy Spirit to them, but since the three persons of the Godhead are all living and moving and sharing in each other, the indwelling involves all three, by the Spirit. So we should not just assume, 'Well, Jesus comes to live in me, the Spirit's out here, the Father's out there!' Nor is it that 'the Father has come to live in me, but where have Jesus and the Spirit gone?' Nor is it just simply that Christ in us is really the Spirit! We are trying to get to grips with a God who cannot be separated by those terms so precisely, because each person of the Godhead is living and dancing and moving in and out of each other all the time. That is why, if you are really letting Christ live in you, or if you ask the Spirit of God to fill you (which you should do every day), or if you are confident that the Father has set up family and is at home within you, then you are going to experience a dynamism within. No matter what deadness you face outside, within you there is life teeming! And that God, who is moving and living within you, dancing around in your life, will keep your heart dancing too.

> My God, I am Thine;
> What a comfort divine,
> What a blessing to know
> That my saviour is mine.
> In the heavenly Lamb
> Thrice blessed I am,
> And my heart it doth dance
> At the sound of His name.

Charles Wesley wrote this hymn after a young servant girl was converted and danced all the way home.

# 4

# The Bosom Friends

The Trinitarian God – Father, Son and Spirit – is a bunch of bosom friends. In this chapter, I want to take up this idea and look at what the Bible says about the friendships between each person of the Godhead. Because this book is about the Trinity, we will not look deeply at this point into the deity of Christ or the deity of the Spirit specifically. Looking at these questions would expand the inquiry too greatly, and I would really need to write a separate book on each person of the Godhead even to begin to do them justice. However, we will inevitably touch on these subjects along the way.

### . . . in the bosom of the Father

John 1:18 tells us that 'no one has seen God at any time'. Pure *God-ness* exists in dimensions that our eyes are not created or equipped to take in – it exists 'multidimensionally', if you like. Pure God-ness is unseeable for humans but, if we want to know what God is like, He has made provision for us. God has taken the trouble to make Himself known in our language and visible in our dimension. When we look at Jesus, we see a man. But Jesus says, 'He who has seen Me has seen the Father' (John 14:9). It is a man we are looking at; we do not see God, we see man.

But somehow, when we see that man, we see the Father. Jesus is the language, the message by which we can see the Godhead. Through Him we can know the otherwise invisible Father.

> No man has seen God at any time; the only-begotten God who is in the bosom of the Father, He has explained Him. (John 1:18)

The Greek word we translate 'only-begotten' is *monogenēs*. The idea could refer to the eternal begetting of the Son from the Father – the eternal generation that goes on within the Godhead. It is not that the Son is created from the Father, but rather eternally generated from the source of the Father's life. But this is not the aspect we are going to pick up on at this point. The contextual idea of the word *monogenēs*, taken from its use in Scripture, means 'unique', or 'one of a kind'. The 'only-begotten God' (some texts may have the 'only-begotten *Son*', but the best Greek texts read 'God'), who is in the bosom of the Father, is completely unique. There is none like Him. He is one of a kind because He has 'explained God'. We could say, 'He has *exegeted* God'. I like the word 'exegeted' as a translation because we derive it directly from the Greek word in the text, and the meaning is 'to take out what is already there so that it can be understood' – that is what exegesis is! We take out what is there in the text in order to make it understandable to others. Thus, Jesus *exegetes* God. He brings forth what is already there in God, without adding to it or taking away from it. He is taken out from God so that we can see what God is like. The 'only-begotten God', who has come out from God, *is* God, and He spells out what God is like, so that although we have never seen God, nonetheless we can know Him.

The only-begotten God is 'in the bosom of the Father'. You cannot really describe a closer relationship than to be 'in somebody's bosom'. Today we might say, 'That friend of mine is in my heart, dear to my heart!' You are as close together as you possibly can be. We still speak of 'bosom friends'. Jesus is the God who is in the bosom of God. He is the God who is the 'feeling' and the 'thinking' of God (*logos*, correctly translated, means not just 'word', but 'faculty of thought'). This is partly what John means earlier when, in John 1, he calls Jesus the 'word who is God'. When you think, you generate your thoughts. What you are thinking is really part of you – it is who you are, it is your thoughts and opinions. They come from your bosom, out of the depths of your heart. Your own thoughts are what are in closest relationship to you, most closely identifiable with you.

God has been generating God through eternity. God has been bringing God out of His bosom; God has been conceiving of thoughts and words for all eternity. The eternal begetting, the eternal generation, never actually began at a particular point in time: that would mean that Jesus was in some way less than the Father – His product. We tend to think that first one has to have a person and then they have some thoughts. But can you really have a person without thoughts? The writer of the Proverbs says,

As he thinks within himself, so he is. (Proverbs 23:7)

Thinking, even if only at a very basic level, begins the moment we come into being. If you take the thought out of a person, what is left? If you take the word out of God, what is left? He would be nothing at all. So, the Son of God is eternally generated from the Father – 'the only-begotten God' from the bosom of the Father.

Similarly, the Spirit is called the Spirit of God. He is sent forth from God (John 14:26), breathed out by God, or is the *spiration* of God (sending breath is *spirating*), because the word 'Spirit' is the same as 'breath'. But the Father, of course, is never called the

'Father of God'. There is one God and Father (Ephesians 4:6). Jesus is called the 'Son of God' because He is God out of God; and the Spirit is the 'Spirit of God' or the 'Spirit of the Father' because He is breathed out of God. The Nicene Creed was trying to express this by saying 'very God of God'. The word 'of' is *ek* in Greek, literally meaning 'out of' – 'very God *out of* God'. Jesus is not just God; He is God out of God. He is the Son of God. The Spirit is not just God; He is Spirit out of God. He is the Spirit of God. This is the beginning of trying to understand the relationships inside the Trinity.

### The 'eternal generator'

It was Origen, the early third-century theologian, who coined the phrase 'the eternal generation of the Son of God'. He recognized that the description of Jesus in John 1:18 as being 'in the bosom of the Father' is very important. Perhaps the closest way we can express this on earth is to put our head on somebody's chest. And that is just what the beloved disciple, John, who captured the phrase in his Gospel, did at the Last Supper – he put his head on Jesus' chest. Jesus and John are as near an analogy as we can see for how the Father and the Son exist in relationship together. Moreover, if John is a Spirit-filled disciple, when he puts his head on Jesus' breast the Spirit inside him also resides there, in the bosom of his friend. And that is also where the Spirit resides in the Godhead. As Christ dwells in the bosom of the Father, so the Spirit dwells in Jesus' breast, and in the bosom of the Father.

Jesus said that 'from his innermost being will flow rivers of living water' (John 7:38). Most of our translations put this in such a way that we interpret it to mean that if we believe in Jesus, rivers of water flow out of our innermost being. This is a possible rendering of the Greek and makes theological sense. But, as in a number of places in John's Gospel, the meaning changes if we punctuate the sentence differently. Greek did not use punctuation in the same way as we do in English, so that different interpretations are often possible on the basis of punctuation. Instead of understanding the second part of the sentence as being contingent on the first – *If* I believe in Jesus *then* the Scripture promises that rivers of living water will flow out of my innermost being – we could understand the second part of the sentence as describing the first – *If* I believe in Jesus, I am believing in the one about whom the Scripture says that '*from his* innermost being living waters will flow'. We could therefore translate:

> If any man is thirsty, let him come to Me; and let him drink, he who believes in Me. As the Scripture has said, 'Out of His innermost being shall flow rivers of living water.'

The prophet Ezekiel predicted that the temple of God would have a river streaming from within it out into the world (Ezekiel 47). Jesus said that He was the fulfilment of the Old Testament temple of God (John 2:19–21). John tells us that the living waters the Scripture prophesied about are the Holy Spirit (John 7:38–9). Therefore, the Holy Spirit streams forth from the innermost places of Jesus, the new temple of God, out into the world as well as into the experiences of our lives (see also Exodus 17:1–6; 1 Corinthians 10:4; Psalm 105:40–1).

The Spirit originates from the Father and is breathed out from the Father to the Son. The Spirit then takes up His residence in the bosom, or the innermost being, of Jesus and flows forth from there into our lives. Literally, the Hebrew for 'innermost being' means something like 'the bowels', but we tend to discard that translation for obvious reasons. In both the Hebrew and Greek languages, the source of compassion was the bowels. When the Gospels record Jesus as being 'moved with compassion', the Greek word *splagchnizomai* literally means something like 'being stirred in his bowels'. Compassion is something that moves your guts. *Splagchnizomai* is only ever used of either God or Jesus, or of Jesus as represented in a parable. It is the love of God being moved from within and flowing out by His Spirit. There is, therefore, a bosom relationship within the Trinity. If Jesus is the 'Word' of God, the Holy Spirit is the 'breath' of God, His 'spiration'. Words and breath are intimately linked. Words are formed breath. The breath is a very intimate part of a person. If you can feel someone's breath, you must be very close to him or her. God lives in His breath, He lives in His Spirit, and the Spirit of God is that which dwells within God, that out of which God lives, and that which exudes from Him, or proceeds from Him.

These are the bosom friendships within God. In John 14:16 and 26, Jesus twice says that the Father will send the Spirit. And then in John 15:26 and John 16:7 He says that He will send the Spirit (although, please note, not necessarily without asking the Father). Finally, when Jesus goes back to heaven, He receives the Spirit from the Father and then pours the Spirit forth (Acts 2:33). So the procession of the Spirit is ultimately always from the Father. It is a bit like Jesus saying in John 15: *You are my friends if you keep my commandments, you are no longer servants. A servant doesn't know what the master is talking about and he just has to do what he is told, but I want a relationship with you which is a friend relationship.*

Why does Jesus make this point? Quite simply, that is the kind of relationship that He enjoys within the Godhead. There is a certain relationship within the Godhead between the Father, His breath and His Word, which may also be described as a relationship between three friends – the three bosom friends of the Trinity.

## Subordination or equality in the Trinity?

Why am I emphasizing friendship within the Trinity? Well, what about the question of subordination within the Trinity? If Jesus is the Son of God, and the Spirit is the Spirit of God, but the Father is not the Father of God, then do they not form some sort of hierarchy? Some theologians talk about the subordination of the Son and the Spirit to the Father. Others say they are subordinate only in the history of creation and the story of humankind and redemption, and that the subordination does not exist within God in eternity. This idea makes a distinction between what is known as the 'economic' Trinity and what is known as the 'ontological' Trinity. 'Ontological', from the Greek *einai*, 'to be', means the essential being: who God is, in essence, for ever. 'Economic' comes from the word *oikos*, which means 'house', and so came to mean the ordering of the household, so to speak: how things are set up for a specific purpose.

The economic Trinity is how the three persons of the Godhead order themselves so as to be expressed in human history. Some proponents of this view of the Trinity would support it by quoting the verses in 1 Corinthians 15:23–8:

> . . . then comes the end, when [Christ] hands over the
> kingdom to the God and Father . . . so that God may
> be all in all.

Proponents of this view believe that, when Jesus comes again, it will no longer be necessary for the Trinity to function 'economically' and at this point the Trinity will again function ontologically. Such theologians tend to have two views of what God is like, one for the present and one for the future:

1) God as He is in revelation and relationship accommodating to us His creatures, and

2)  God as He is really in His being for ever.

I am not overly satisfied with this definition of the 'economic' Trinity, for it reduces our view of revelation. If God has been revealed to us in Christ (and indeed He has), then that revelation *must* be of His eternal condition and nature – otherwise it is not revealing much to us but is a sort of pragmatic façade for the current situation. If there is an element of subordination within the Trinity, then it must be part of the ontological, essential, eternal and unchanging character of God expressed in time and space through Jesus and His relationship with the Father. Thus it is significant that it was the second person of the Trinity who became human, and it is significant that it was the third person who is poured out among us. Each person of the Trinity has an essential, ontological function – not only in human history, but also within the being of this one God. We will look more closely at the nature of subordination within the Trinity and its role in Church history later in this chapter (see also chapter six, under 'Judaism'), but first I want to continue to emphasize the equality of the persons of the Godhead as they relate in bosom friendship.

## Humility in the Trinity

Although the Father is, in one sense, the source or the origin of the Son and Spirit (remembering, as we have said, that this means eternally sourcing, eternally originating), nevertheless they are, in another sense, equal to one another. There is nothing missing of God when we look at Christ, for:

> In Him all the fullness of deity dwells in bodily form.
> (Colossians 2:9)

Christ is not deficient in His revelation of God. This is called *christocentric* theology – not Jesus-centric, but christocentric.

Christocentric means that our understanding of God centres on the revelation of God the Son as the Anointed Messiah (the Greek *christos* means 'the anointed one'). Jesus was anointed with the Holy Spirit, and thus it is Christ, the Anointed One, who shows us all the ontological and essential nature of God here in time and space. The way that each person of the Trinity functions shows that they are equals – we come to the Father through Jesus (John 14:6), a relationship made available to us by the Holy Spirit within us witnessing that we are children of God (Romans 8:16). Moreover, each person of the Trinity submits and gives way to the other at different times (see also Jesus in Gethsemane: 'If possible, let this cup pass from Me; yet not My will, but Yours be done').

The Trinity is a wonderful expression of humility: three equal friends who, nonetheless, give way to one another in the manner of a servant. Jesus says He can do nothing of Himself unless He sees the Father doing it (John 5:19). The Spirit does not speak on His own initiative, but only what He hears from the Godhead (John 16:13). Jesus prays that His Father would glorify Him with the glory He enjoyed before the world existed, a glory equal with His Father's (John 17:5). Thus, within God from eternity, the idea of obedience, humility and servanthood has continually existed before God even created the world. Unless we have a Trinitarian God, we can't have a humble God – at least not one who has been humble from eternity. If we go around preaching that everyone should be a servant and must begin by serving a monotheistic, non-Trinitarian God, ultimately we are creatures who can never be like God in respect to our need to submit and obey. But it is our chief end as human beings to become, in Christ, like God. If God himself is a servant in the very essence of His being, and He is, then we may truly become like Him.

The fundamental lie that the devil tempts humanity to believe is that we can be like God by asserting our own will and disobeying Him. But we can't be like God by disobeying Him. God is perfect obedience. The Father rejoiced that the Son said, *Not My will, but Yours be done* in the garden of Gethsemane; God the Father is thrilled when He sends forth His Spirit and the Spirit says, *Yes, I will go.*

The devil lies and tells us that God does not want us to be like Him. But it is God's command to us to be like Him and follow the example of Christ,

> who, although He existed in the form of God, did not regard equality with God a thing to be grasped, but emptied Himself, taking the form of a bondservant. (Philippians 2:7)

Within the being of God there is the fundamental, unchangeable principle of obedience and humility. Where else in the universe can you find a God like that? He didn't just play-act at being a servant for a few years; He has always been a servant. That is why we aspire to be obedient and give way to each other, because this is what God is like. Our Trinitarian theology affects our daily behaviour.

So, the Son of God is eternally generated; but we do not say that the Spirit of God is generated. Origen was prepared to say this, but other theologians decided that this was not the best way of expressing it. It is better to say that the Spirit of God *proceeds*, or is *sent forth* from the Father. 'Spirit' and 'breath' are the same word, so it can be said that the Spirit is 'breathed out' from the Father. The technical word is 'spirated' (we only have this word in common usage as 'aspirate': to exhale or breathe out, and 'inspire': to inhale or breathe in). When I *breathe* on you, you are affected by me. When I *generate* something, I produce a bit of me and push it out to you over there! All of God is being *generated* all the time out of the Father in Christ. All of God is being *breathed* out of the Father all the time in His Spirit.

A simple young man of little education spoke of this great doctrine of the Trinity:

> Three in one and one in three,
> and the middle one died for me.

Irenaeus, an Early Church father who came before the great Trinitarian theologians known as the Cappadocian fathers, summed up the Trinity very simply by saying that the Son and the Spirit are like the two hands of God. I like this picture, so long as we remember that whenever God does something, He does it with both hands! The Father, Son and Spirit are always involved together in the activity of God. You can't cut off either of His hands and still find God – He and His hands go together to make up the whole God. Some people's hands tell you all about their heart. You can look at what a person is doing with their hands and understand what is in his or her heart. That is why we like holding some people's hands and not others. Everything about God's heart is conveyed in His two hands.

### A historical dispute

At this point I must make mention of the *Filioque* controversy. *Filioque* is a compound Latin word meaning 'and from the Son'. The Niceno-Constantinopolitan Creed (AD 381) states that 'the Holy Spirit proceeds from the Father'. All of the different orthodox denominations of the Church in the fourth century agreed that the Nicene Creed was a good, biblically accurate statement of the fundamental truths of Christianity – and so it is. That does not mean that we might not want to develop or deepen our understanding of it at times, as theology develops over the centuries. Some Anabaptists in the Reformation were charged with being non-Trinitarian because they wanted to look behind the creeds to get back to how the Early Church fathers formulated these statements. I think that charge is unfair. They did not necessarily disagree with the creed or contradict it; they just wanted to see if they could find a better or deeper way of expressing the truths. People do much the same today. They try to find new terms through which to express truth. But nonetheless, we should be careful not to dismiss these early thinkers and their words. We do not always get any nearer to the truth by being more fastidious or superior.

After the Nicene Creed had been agreed, the Latin Western Church thought they would state it better. Unfortunately, their statement leads to the idea that within the Trinity there was not only a subordination of the Son and the Spirit to the Father, but also that the Spirit was subordinate to the Son. Thus they created a kind of hierarchy within the Trinity: the Father is the governor, then the Son is His second in command and the Spirit is at the beck and call of both! So, without consulting the Council of Churches, the Western Church added the *Filioque* clause, so that the statement about the Spirit read, 'the Holy Spirit proceeds from the Father *and the Son*'. Understandably, there was some bad feeling from the Eastern Greek Church about this change being made without proper consultation, and after everything had been agreed by all. It led eventually to the divergence of the two church streams in the eleventh century, in both theology and relationship. It could be argued that the result of the *Filioque* amendment in Western theology was that the Spirit was relegated to a less significant role in the Godhead, and thus the gifts, ministries and manifestations of the Spirit were seldom experienced in much of Western church life. The Pentecostal Church and the charismatic movement have done much to restore the importance of the Holy Spirit in Western theology, although He is still seen to be less relevant in some theological streams.

This is the kind of wrong emphasis that Irenaeus avoided with his picture of the two hands of God. The Bible gives us no such lower view of the Spirit. Jesus and the Spirit go hand in hand in the person of Christ, the one anointed by the Spirit of the sovereign Lord. Every work of Christ was a work of the Spirit, every act was done in the power of the Spirit – so too should Christian lives be! Thus the persons of the Trinity dwell together, enjoying the equality and mutual submission of bosom friends.

# 5

# The 'Triple Helix' God

This short chapter specifically addresses those with scientific and mathematical inclinations and draws from contemporary biological models. However, I encourage even those without such inclinations to persist with these initial thoughts, since they help us to understand an aspect of the Trinity that has often been neglected. The language of theology has always been predominantly masculine and many have pushed, quite rightly, for more to be discovered about the feminine within God. This model of the Godhead as a three-stranded cord makes an important contribution to our understanding of the Trinitarian concept, as it engages the matter of gender and masculine and feminine disposition. We need, therefore, to examine it seriously. (For more on the issue of masculinity and femininity in church life, please see the book, *Women and the Kingdom*, co-written with my wife Faith Forster.) We will develop this idea using the image of DNA, the building block of all life.

In Genesis 1:26–7 we read:

> Then God said, 'Let Us make man in Our image, according to Our likeness' . . . God created man in His own image, in the image of God He created him; male and female He created them.

In this passage use of the Hebrew *'Elohiym*, plural of *'elowahh*, meaning 'deity', hints at plurality, at some level, in the Godhead. Here, God seems to indicate two dimensions to His intent in creating humankind. The first, 'in Our image' (from *tselem*), means 'shadow', or 'phantom', and suggests that we (as humankind) are *representative of* the Trinity. The second, 'after Our own likeness' (from *demuwth*), indicates a more concrete *resemblance*, shape or model, possibly referring to the character and disposition of the Trinity in relationship (ie, the dimensions of masculinity and femininity). Of course, God is not *male* or *female* as He does not have gender, but as we shall see He does express Himself as both masculine and feminine. As such, male and female are both created in His image. The male gender normally expresses more of the masculine characteristics of God and, generally speaking, the female gender carries more of the feminine.

We all have both masculine and feminine characteristics within us, and biologically the only distinction between a male and a female is the Y chromosome, the smallest of our 46 chromosomes of DNA.

This idea of the 'triple helix' is, of course, an allusion to the famous double helix of DNA: the building block of life discovered by James Watson and Francis Crick in 1953. The double helix comprises two chains of nucleotides that look like a spiral zip. Bases protrude from each chain like teeth and pair up together with the other row, to form an exact match. The final zip carries, through this sequence of bases, a language that will pass on information accurately when the DNA is unzipped. The language, called code, contains the blueprint for biological life, but, with the exception of identical twins, each individual's genetic code is unique. (The whole human genome, comprises approximately 3 million bases per strand, one from each parent, so a human cell contains a total of around 6 billion DNA bases, or in computer terms around 6 gigabytes of data.)

While DNA is a molecular double helix, there is in fact a third 'strand' to the cord – the *message* that is contained in the code: a matched pair of molecules that, when combined, make a unique whole conveying the third element, *the code itself*. This is strangely 'Trinitarian', one might say. The double/triple helix model might, therefore, help us to get an understanding of Trinitarian life. For the scientifically inclined, the remarkable thing is that the four nucleotide bases are able only to bind in two sets of pairs, A:T or T:A and G:C or C:G, which means that God was well ahead of the twenty-first century and its technological explosion of the digital age: infinite potential messages consisting in the simplicity of an on or off, yes or no, right or wrong. Furthermore, the genetic 'alphabet', or codons, comprise bases in blocks of three in which the code is read (eg AAA, ATA, CGT, GAT and so on). Trinitarianism seems, therefore, to be the very cornerstone of life itself.

The motif that DNA offers has an elegance that speaks of the complexity and majesty of the Godhead as expressed in the very foundation of biological life. The three persons of the Godhead relate together in a triple helix structure, spiralling around each other like a threefold chord. Ecclesiastes 4:12 reminds us that such a chord cannot easily be broken. That model helps us to think about God as fundamental to life, bringing forth that which cannot easily be changed or broken. Given what can be expressed in 6 gigabytes of DNA and the millions of species on earth, (in 2003, the 'Species 2000' project had identified over 300,000 species of moss alone!), imagine what myriad of revelation, what depths lie within a spiritual triple helix, reflecting our infinitely complex God who lies behind our very complex universe. The rationalists and scientists among us might express the Trinity in these sorts of terms. Nevertheless, although the model emphasizes *life*, it doesn't actually convey the *personhood* that we see in the biblical revelation of Father, Son and Spirit. Going back to the double helix, let us then re-examine the third element of the 'message'.

The message is what runs through the whole structure of the being and informs it, or defines it, to make it the kind of person it is. This is where we see the feminine aspect of God brought out. The Father breathes out the Spirit from eternity. 'Spirit', or 'breath', is the word *ruach* in Hebrew, which is a feminine noun – similarly, the 'dove' image of the New Testament is a female image for the Spirit (of course, the gender of a noun does not insist that the object is male or female – God is, as I have said, neither, but is both masculine and feminine from eternity, and humanity reflects the Godhead through the image of male and female, masculine and feminine). So we have the masculine Father, out of whom comes the feminine Spirit, just as in Genesis 2 God brought the woman out of man. In the Godhead, the fusion of the two persons in this eternal relationship (like the two strands that constitute DNA) perhaps could be seen to generate the message (*logos*), who is Christ. This model, therefore, can help us to picture how the Spirit has a part to play, with the Father, in the eternal generation of the Son. The message is what determines or defines the whole person.

This seems to me to be a helpful way of thinking about the Trinity for the twenty-first-century mind. It is certainly interesting to be able to demonstrate both the masculine and the feminine characteristics of God. This is something we read about in the Bible, and yet seldom articulate in our theology. We see God likening Himself to a mother as Jesus mourns over Jerusalem (Luke 13:34), and as God promises a mother's faithfulness to His people (Isaiah 49:15). Within God there is a generative process that happens through the interaction of the persons of the Godhead relating from eternity. Humanity reflects the Godhead through the image of male and female, masculine and feminine.

Father and Spirit make possible the concept of the Son, who carries the divine genetic code, bringing the message into the world. Hence it is the Word of God who came to the earth to communicate and bring forth the truth of who the person of God is. Philo, a Greek Jew who was an early philosopher and theologian, and who believed the Old Testament, understood the Trinitarian relationship in another way. As a Jew he only trusted the Old Testament and did not accept the Christian view of the Trinity; he therefore found it difficult to understand why God is represented by three persons who visit Abraham in Genesis 18. The three persons are addressed as a singular. It would appear from Genesis 18 that the three men are a symbol, or are figurative, of the Trinitarian God. Philo came up with this analogy to avoid Judaistically unacceptable tritheism: when light shines down on an object from two directions, the one object casts two shadows. The object cannot exist without the shadows, nor the shadows without the object. He explained Abraham's visitation in terms of God with two shadows (Philo, *A Treatise on the Life of the Wise Man Made Perfect by Instruction, or On the Unwritten Law, That is to Say, On Abraham*, p. xxiv). The analogy is not strong in some ways – it does not explain the need for such a threefold representation of God, and it is difficult to see what the light would be, shining on our revelation of God. But it does have something in common with our double/triple helix picture. Both help us to see the relationships within the Trinity as being in some way codependent: the helix, because the fusing together of the structure causes the organic life; and the shadows, because they cannot exist without the original.

However we choose to look at it, we can conclude that the relationships within the Trinity are real relationships. The Trinity is not a random collection of beings who like to stick together; it is not a relationship of three like objects built together into cohesion. Somehow, rather, the relationship between them is symbiotic, necessary for the life of the whole being of God.

# 6

# Defending Trinitarianism

I touched briefly upon some of the opponents to Trinitarian doctrine in the introduction, and we will pick up on these further in this chapter. It is increasingly important in our current cultural climate to learn how to answer the attacks on the fundamental assertions of our faith, so that we can stand confidently and preach the truth in a pluralistic society. We will tackle the opponents and their objections under eight different categories.

## The Sceptics

I remember my intellectual schoolmaster, to whom I owe a lot for introducing me to life in all sorts of new areas, saying to me one day, 'I can never understand what on earth the theologians are talking about when they go on about the Trinity!' That is how he dismissed it. He appeared not to have had much religious instruction – the limit of it extended to a comment he made to me on another occasion: 'Blessed are those who expect nothing, for they shall not be disappointed'!

In the last few centuries, atheistic and sceptical intellectuals have emerged who think that they are being analytically robust when they dismiss the Trinity as something of a waste of time.

They happily write it off as an intellectual nonsense. Before I quote one or two of them, let me just contrast this modern sceptical period with the fourth century and, in particular, the time of the three men known as the 'Cappadocian fathers', who built on the earlier work of Athanasius and the Nicene Creed (Athanasius' contribution to Trinitarian theology was groundbreaking; he even suffered exile by the Emperor for his defence of the doctrine).

This trio, Gregory of Nazianzus, Basil of Caesarea and his brother Gregory of Nyssa, keep cropping up in connection with the doctrine of the Trinity because they defended the Trinity against the attacks of the Arians (who denied the deity of Christ and the Spirit). The debate raged through all sections of society in the fourth century. Gregory of Nyssa said famously of that period:

> If you ask for change, someone philosophizes to you
> on the begotten and un-begotten. If you ask the price
> of bread, you are told the Father is greater and the Son
> inferior. And if you ask if the bath is ready, someone
> answers that the Son was created from nothing. (*On
> the Deity of the Son and the Holy Spirit*, p. xlvi, 557b)

The Greek and Roman world in the fourth century was buzzing with theological inquiry and thought. How different from our situation today in the twenty-first century! It is very rare to find the person on the street engaged in those kinds of discussions today. If, as I have said, theology is the queen of the sciences, then somehow we have lost our ability to put across the deep and wonderful truths in a meaningful way, so that they stick in the vocabulary of ordinary people. But they were able to do this in the fourth century – ordinary people were talking about deep theology.

By the time we get to the eighteenth century, however, the philosopher Immanuel Kant was saying:

> The doctrine of the Trinity, taken literally, has no practical relevance at all, even if we think we understand it; and it is even more clearly irrelevant if we realize that it transcends all our concepts. Whether we are to worship three or ten persons in the Deity makes no difference . . . no difference in rules of conduct. (*The Conflict of the Faculties* (trans. M. J. Gregor), pp. 65, 67)

Another such sceptic was Thomas Jefferson, the nineteenth-century American president, who felt particularly irritated by the complexities of 'Trinitarian arithmetic': $1 + 1 + 1 = 3$. (He apparently never tried $1 \times 1 \times 1 = 1$!) He stated:

> When we shall have done away with the incomprehensible jargon of the Trinitarian arithmetic, that three are one, and one is three; when we shall have knocked down the artificial scaffolding, reared to mask from view the very simple structure of Jesus; when, in short, we shall have unlearned everything which has been taught since His day, and got back to the pure and simple doctrines He inculcated, we shall then be truly and worthily His disciples. (Quoted in Christopher Hall, 'Adding Up the Trinity', in *Christianity Today* 41.5 (1997), p. 26)

That is how much he thought of the Trinity. In the twentieth century Roderick Leupp, trying to sum up the current atmosphere of the church climate in which he moved, wrote:

> For most people and, sadly, for most Christians also, the Trinity is the great unknown. The Trinity, to use a familiar equation is viewed as a riddle wrapped up inside a puzzle and buried in an enigma. A riddle, for how can any entity be at the same time multiple (three)

yet singular (one)? A puzzle, for the Trinity is so clearly contrary to any rational thought as not to warrant a second thought from sensible people. An enigma, for even if the Trinity could be understood, of what practical value, even what religious value, would it have for ordinary people? (in *Knowing the Name of God: A Trinitarian Tapestry of Grace, Faith and Community*)

And again, Karl Rahner, a contemporary Catholic theologian, in a book about the Trinity noted that:

Despite their orthodox confession of the Trinity, Christians are, in their practical life, almost mere monotheists. (*The Trinity*, trans. J. Donceel, p. 10)

This may all sound a bit depressing. But, on the other hand, I can think of at least twelve fairly significant works written on the Trinity over the last ten years by academic theologians (see the Bibliography). After years and years of not very much being written or said, theologians are beginning to talk about the Trinity again. It is no longer an embarrassing doctrine. People are discussing the Trinity on a rational level and some of their books are very readable, as well as being scholarly and thoughtful. There is a Trinitarian revival going on in academic circles. Here are one or two positive remarks:

The Trinitarian doctrine is the immediate implication of the fact, form and content of biblical revelation. (Donald Bloesch, *God the Almighty*)

And Alister McGrath has commented that the Trinitarian God is simply the believer's final word about the God whom he knows, loves and adores.

Let me reflect on that word 'love' for a moment. When you love someone, don't you want to understand them? Even if you have loved your husband or wife for many years, you still can't tell me that you know *everything* about them yet! Getting to know or understand someone goes on for ever, in a sense. But just because it is impossible to put a box around someone and say, 'I know this person inside out and completely now – I don't need to know any more!' doesn't mean that the pursuit is worthless. Love wants to go on finding out about its object. Worship is the means by which we invade the heart of God and understand whatever depths we can, even if we know that we are never going to have a final statement that will sum up everything in a neat little bundle. We will not understand everything about God simply because we have formulated two or three definitive statements about Him.

Again, Professor Torrance has written concerning the revival of interest in the Trinity that today it has a vibrancy and a vitality that have been unknown in the field since the stormy days of the fourth century.

I can feel that vibrancy; can you? It is the Son of God sharing His love for the Father with *us*, through the Spirit. The doctrine of the Trinity is truly important because God is personal, He is communal, He is loving, He is altruistic – and He is all of those things for ever and ever. These truths have a lot of bearing on how we see ourselves and how we seek to function in our earthly relationships together.

'Self-giving love is the Trinity's signature,' says Leupp in *Knowing the Name of God*. That is lovely, isn't it? He is not a self-contained, egotistical and self-absorbed God, as theology has sometimes presented Him. God's love is another reason we should not dismiss the doctrine of the Trinity as irrelevant.

The sceptics, some of whom we have just quoted, often base their attacks on the premise that the deity of Christ, and the deity of the Spirit, were ideas born out of the debates of the fourth century. They maintain that before that time there was no real talk of the Trinity in Christian theology, and that the doctrine arose out of fanciful accretions added from later philosophies. Thus, in their view, the Trinity bears no relation to the simple teachings of Jesus, from which Christian theology has since all but departed. It can be dismissed either as an irrelevance for the Christian's everyday life, or as an irrational belief that cannot be justified by the earliest roots of Christian doctrine. The sceptics would argue that, through the growth and development of Christian theology which we have discussed, this warped and impotent doctrine of the Trinity has sprung up.

The sceptics are wrong, however, as we can easily prove by a quick look at some of the early Christian writings, including Paul's first and second letters to the Thessalonians, as we looked at in chapter 1. It is therefore surprising that this view is still being put forward in a number of television and radio programmes, as well as popular magazines and books. The fourth-century Cappadocian fathers were engaging in a debate over the Trinity on the basis of foundations that had already been laid by Early Church fathers in previous centuries, going right back to the first Christians.

Polycarp, who sat at the feet of John the Apostle, very clearly saw Christ as God; as did Ignatius, who was a second-century apologist. II Clement was a second century apologetic writing (unrelated to I Clement, as far as we can tell), which states that 'we must think of Jesus as we think of God' (II Clement 1:1). Irenaeus, from the mid-second century, was the first bishop of the Celts. He came from Smyrna, where he had known Polycarp and studied under him, only one generation away from John the Apostle. As we have seen, Irenaeus was the man who came up with the analogy of the Son and the Spirit as the two hands of God reaching into creation and effecting redemption.

The second-century philosopher Justin Martyr was also Trinitarian, in that he worshipped the Father, Son and Spirit, while subordinating the Son (the 'eternal Logos') and the Spirit in his understanding of the way God functioned. He was a man who died for his faith. He was a clear, concise thinker who had examined all the philosophies of his time and used to debate continuously in Rome with the philosophers there. He was in no way weak in reason or easily misled into error. Eventually, the other philosophers were so defeated by him that they decided it was time he should die – hence his name.

Tertullian, at the end of the second century, was clearly Trinitarian. Indeed, he invented the word 'Trinity' in order to put a name to this line of thinking that had its origins in the days of the earliest Christians (see for example *Against Praxeas*, chapter two and *passim*). At the very beginning of the second century a non-Christian Roman governor, Pliny the Younger, had written to the Emperor Hadrian concerning his first encounter with Christians. 'I have never participated in trials of Christians,' he wrote. 'I therefore do not know what offences it is the practice to punish or investigate, and to what extent.' In the letter he also includes a fascinating account taken from the Christians that he had imprisoned and tortured. This account explains how, early in the morning before the dawn broke, before the sun arose, they met together and there they worshipped Jesus: 'they sang a hymn to Christ as God' (*Letters*, 10.96–7).

Other emerging Trinitarians include Athenagoras and the writers of the 'Epistle of Barnabas' and the 'Shepherd of Hermas' – all in the second century – and Hippolytus, at the very beginning of the third century. All of these treated the Godhead – Father, Son and Holy Spirit – as a unity, because they believed in one God, a 'monarchical oneness', as it is sometimes called. In the third century, Origen made his contribution of the theory of the Son's subordination to the Father. It was men like these, trying to sum up the biblical revelation of God, reinforced by their own experiential knowledge of Him, who paved the way for the later debates that brought the doctrine of the Trinity under the microscope.

The arguments of the sceptics that Jesus was only elevated into the Godhead at a later date are, therefore, completely unfounded. Any historian would demonstrate that it is incorrect to assert that the 'mapping process', as theology grows and develops and becomes more precise, has meant that Jesus, who began as 'a good rabbi' or 'an outstanding kind of man', gradually became a 'God' by the fourth century and part of a 'Trinity' that suddenly came into existence. These kinds of arguments have gained some popularity in the twentieth and twenty-first centuries but, unless you are familiar with the Early Church fathers, you cannot begin to refute them.

The eighteenth-century period known as the Enlightenment gave rise to the charge that we had 'made God in our own image', rather than Him making us in His – that the whole thing was merely a human creation and incomprehensible theology. How strange, then, that the image of God we have created is so complicated and complex that we would have to dismiss Him for being unreasonable and impossible to believe in! We should be ready to answer such specious arguments.

I believe there to be what I have just called a 'mapping process', as we come to know our God and try to describe Him better. Basil of Caesarea (one of the Cappadocian fathers we mentioned earlier) has sometimes been called an 'innovator' for his contribution concerning the person of the Holy Spirit. This is because, up until his day, discussion had been focused mainly on the Father and the Son – especially defending the truth that

Jesus is God from heretical attack. Little work had been done (in terms of theology, that is) on the person of the Spirit. In Basil's time, however, there were heretics saying that the Spirit was a 'creature', a created being. And so, against these charges, Basil gathered what was already implicit, and at times explicit, from Bible texts, Church history and the ordinary experience of believers up until that time. He insisted that the Spirit had to be honoured with the Son in equal measure. He made mention of the phrase 'Holy, Holy, Holy' that the cherubim sing to the Lord in Isaiah 6:3. The 'Holies' are undifferentiated. You could say that they are three 'Holies' of equal honour, one for each person of the Trinity, and yet they are still one word: 'Holy'. He also picked up on the *Gloria*, which the Church had been using since early times: 'Glory be to the Father, and to the Son and to the Holy Spirit'. He emphasized that the persons of the Godhead are equal, and that neither the Son nor the Spirit is inferior. Basil was not bringing in anything new. As we have seen, this is the way we try to understand the revelation our God has given us of Himself. We put our experience, our biblical exegesis and our reason on a map, in our journey deeper into understanding the truth of the nature of God. We will not come up with anything *new* – any extra revelation that has not been there since the beginning of the Church – but we will be able to understand our God better and to love Him more deeply.

Let me finish this section by quoting the Cappadocian father Gregory of Nazianzus. He drew on all of the Early Church theology that had gone before, and that we have just begun to look at, when he summed up the wonder of Trinitarian inquiry as follows:

> I cannot think of the One without immediately being surrounded by the radiance of the Three. Nor can I discern the Three without at once being carried back

> to the One. When I think of any One of the Three I think of Him as the Whole, and my vision is filled, and the greater part of what I am thinking of escapes me. I cannot grasp the greatness of That One so as to attribute a greater greatness to the Rest. Then I contemplate the Three together and I see but One luminary, and I cannot divide or measure out the Undivided Light. (*The Oration on Holy Baptism*, preached at Constantinople on 6 Jan 381, being the day following the delivery of that on the Holy Lights, p. XLI)

With these words he attempted to express his experience, his reason and his philosophy, together with his ability to exegete Scripture.

### The Unitarians (Deists)

Unitarianism is the belief that God exists in one person, not three. Groups that adhere to such teaching include the Jehovah's Witnesses and the Christadelphians. The roots of this form of attack on Trinitarianism come largely from within the Church itself and go back to the eighteenth century. One of the fruits of the eighteenth-century Enlightenment is the emphasis upon the *individual* in popular philosophy and social ethics. This means that when we talk about three *persons* in one, we immediately think about three *individuals* in one. This is not really the way that the Early Church understood the word 'person' (Latin *persona*). They did not conceive of a person who was not in relationship with another person – the definition of a person was to be in relationship. People do not exist in isolation, as we saw above when considering the existence of God as a singular being. A single person makes no sense, and cannot fully understand himself or express all that it is to be human if he does not have other human beings to relate to. When we talk about the Trinity, we do not mean to convey a picture of three fully independent, self-sufficient, autonomous and independent persons. That is an Enlightenment assumption, and it is sometimes hard to rid ourselves of it.

A Unitarian god is normally a deistic god – a logical necessity of the human mind rather than one known by revelation, and one who exists miles away from his creation. He set the whole thing up and then left it to its own devices. This idea goes with an eighteenth- and nineteenth-century view of science – a clockwork universe ticking on where God has left it from the beginning of time. Unitarianism reduces Jesus out of the Godhead, saying that He existed simply as a man, or an angel, or had different forms. The Christadelphians were a product of the Enlightenment and could only believe that Jesus began His existence here on earth. Therefore, He was simply a man who could teach good things. But let's go back to the Bible to see what it has to say about such ideas. John 14 describes the relationship between God and Jesus.

> Do not let your heart be troubled; believe in God, believe also in Me. (John 14:1)

Many commentators have pointed out in different ways that there are four possible understandings of this phrase, 'believe also in Me':

(This particular method is not original but one I picked up many years ago. Unfortunately, I cannot now remember its source so as to give proper acknowledgement. I hope the person concerned will forgive me and accept this note as a sign of my indebtedness and gratitude to them!)

1) We could understand the second phrase 'disjunctively', as something new and separate from the first phrase. There is God to be believed in and, separately, there is also Jesus to be believed in. The 'also' is a disjunctive. It shows that there is plurality (at least a duality) in God: the Son and

73

the Father. Therefore the object of our faith is not simply 'God'. As Christians we are believers in God and 'also in Me'. Christian faith binds together a belief that 'there is something out there' with a belief in Jesus and His claims about Himself and what He came to do. Lots of people believe in God but they are not, strictly speaking, Christians until they believe also in Jesus.

2) We could understand the second phrase 'adjunctively', as something similar and additional – a second concept that follows on from the first. The Son is the natural addition to believe in after the Father. Jesus is not only distinct from God, a separate person to believe in, but He is a common object of our faith – 'believe also in Me'. Belief in God and belief in Jesus are brought together, side by side.

3) We could understand the second phrase 'sequentially', in sequence after the first phrase. Number one: 'Believe in God', number two: 'believe also in Me'. There is an order to our faith.

4) Finally, we could understand the second phrase 'conjunctively', joining the two parts together to make a whole. It is a joining of the Father to the Son. 'Believe in God, believe also in Me.' It is another expression of verse 10, 'Do you not believe that I am in the Father and the Father is in Me?' This conjunctive use of the word 'also' is to say that the Father and the Son are 'in' each other. 'I am in the Father and the Father is in Me.' 'The words that I say to you, I do not speak on My own initiative, but the Father abiding in Me does His works.' Thus there is a unity, a coming together, as the Father and the Son cohere within each other.

Understanding God in a Unitarian sense is certainly not a Christian view, as we can see even from the simple words of Jesus at the beginning of John 14. In fact, this simple passage reveals a complex truth when we pull it to pieces and then put it together again. It is an adjunctive, disjunctive, sequential and conjunctive relationship that exists between the Father and the Son.

This relationship is also expressed in the word 'abiding'. 'The Father abides in Me and I abide in the Father.' In fact, you will find this eighteen times in John's Gospel. John 14:2 says 'In My Father's house are many *dwelling places*.' The word 'dwelling place' there comes from the word 'to abide'; we could translate it 'many abodes', or 'many abiding places'. 'I go to prepare an abiding place for you and I will come again.' I do not believe that refers to the second coming, but rather that Jesus is talking about coming back to them in the resurrection. In John 2:16 we read that 'the Father's house' is the temple. But then Jesus interprets the temple as His body: 'Destroy this temple and in three days I will raise it up' (John 2:19). Jesus Himself is the Father's house, where His Father dwells: 'I am in the Father and the Father is in Me!' (John 14:10). The truly incredible thing is that He wants us to share in that divine abiding:

> You will know that I am in My Father, and you in Me
> and I in you. (John 14:20)

Because He wants us to share in the abiding of the Father and Son, He is going away to make an abiding place for us. He does it by the very wounds of Calvary, through which we may be grafted into Himself, the Vine; and by the power of the resurrection, which flows like sap through us, the branches. He has gone away to make a way in which we can come and abide in Him. So, just as the Father and Son cohere and live in a common life, so He is making room now for us to come and share the divine life. Jesus is making space for us within the interactions and movements of the relationships of the Trinity, so that we can all abide together in the life and love of God.

Christians are not just 'brushed and polished-up' human beings; we are those who share the very life of God. We are 'partakers of the divine nature' (2 Peter 1:4). In the upper room at the Last Supper, in the final chapters of his Gospel, John describes to us how Jesus talked to the Father about the disciples as they listened in. It is almost like His practical example of the truths of abiding together that He has been talking about in chapters 14–16. It was as though Jesus, as He prayed, was reaching out His arms around the disciples and pulling them right into the conversation. He said (John 17:6):

> Father . . . I have manifested Your name [ie, 'Father']
> to the men whom You gave Me out of the world; they
> were Yours and You gave them to Me, and they have
> kept Your word.

As Jesus talked intimately to the Father, the disciples were brought into the flow of the communion between the Father and the Son. The description pushes the message home to us: we can share in the house of God, abiding in the communication of the Father and the Son. That is where we are meant to live, so that we can hear the heartbeat of the Trinity as they talk to one another. We are wrapped up within the flow: *Abide in Me and I will abide in you as the Father abides in Me, and we will come and live with you, and abide with you. The Spirit will come and He will abide with you. The Father will come and make His abode with you.* We can live within that life of the Godhead – the concept of the Trinity makes room for us to share the divine life. Unitarianism has no space for that wonderful destiny.

**The Arians (Jehovah's Witnesses)**

The third group of opponents are the Arians. The Jehovah's Witnesses share this theology, as do the now largely discontinued Worldwide Church of God (some will remember the magazine *Plain Truth*, which used to circulate the world), founded by the late H. W. Armstrong. After he died, many followers from the London group asked for teachers to come and teach them about the Trinity. So, although this heresy is popular in some areas, there is also movement away from it.

Armstrong had seen Jesus merely as a good teacher and (like the Jehovah's Witnesses) as an angel, who therefore had a beginning, and who was then sent to earth. This is not a new heresy – in fact, it goes all the way back to a man called Arius, in the fourth century, who taught that Jesus was a created being. His (famous) phrase was, 'there was when He was not', implying a 'beginning' to the Son of God. The Jehovah's Witnesses have revived this ancient heresy in modern times.

The controversy was, and still is, centred around whether Jesus is a created being or not. The verse that had the most relevance in the fourth-century debate, so that it became quite renowned, was in Proverbs 8. This passage is all about Wisdom, who in Proverbs is clearly presented to us as a person. Wisdom personified is female. If we go back to Proverbs 1, we find:

> Wisdom shouts in the street,
> She lifts her voice in the square;
> At the head of the noisy streets she cries out;
> At the entrance of the gates in the city she utters her
> sayings.
> (Proverbs 1:20–1)

The first place in the Scriptures where we confront the idea of 'pouring out the Spirit' is two verses later, in Proverbs 1:23, where Wisdom declares:

> Behold, I will pour out my spirit on you;
> I will make my words known to you.

The spirit of prophecy, who is the Holy Spirit (Acts 2:18), is first introduced to us in Proverbs as the Spirit belonging to Wisdom. The Spirit is in relation to Wisdom and Wisdom is in relation to God. Here, then, we have this personification of Wisdom in female form. And now, in Proverbs 8:22–3, we come to the crux of the matter. Wisdom is speaking, and she says:

> The LORD possessed me at the beginning of His way,
> Before His works of old.
> From everlasting I was established,
> From the beginning, from the earliest times of the earth.

The passage goes on to give a beautiful description of the creation of the universe and then, in verses 30 and 31, Wisdom states:

> I was beside Him, as a master workman;
> And I was daily His delight,
> Rejoicing always before Him,
> Rejoicing in the world, His earth,
> And having my delight in the sons of men.

And these are the verses (mainly v22) that Arius and his followers went to, at the end of the third century and early in the fourth century, to try and prove their case that God was not a Trinity, but that Jesus was a created being, an angel, who was sent to earth to do the redemptive work for humankind.

Is that what these verses really say? Well, first let's tackle the issue of whether or not they are referring to Jesus. It's not too difficult to identify 'Wisdom' with 'Word'. John 1:1 states,

> In the beginning was the Word, and the Word was with God, and the Word was God.

In fact, you could almost say, 'In the beginning was the *Wisdom*, and the *Wisdom* was with God, and the *Wisdom* was God.' Wisdom is clearly presented in Proverbs 8 as having been with God 'from the beginning of His way', which (as we shall see in a moment) is a rather quaint way of saying 'from eternity'. And Wisdom was involved in the creation as a 'master workman'. 1 Corinthians 1 verses 24 and 30 talk of Christ 'the wisdom of God' and Christ who 'became to us wisdom'.

What about the fact that Wisdom personified is female? Well, interestingly enough, when we get to Revelation chapter one, with its glorious picture of Jesus – emphasizing His deity, since the Son of Man is now identified with the Ancient of Days of Daniel 7:9, 13 and 14 – the two figures have been brought together as one. The Son of Man with the white hair of the Ancient of Days (Revelation 1:14), the wise God who possesses the wisdom of eternity – it also says that He is 'girded across His breast with a golden sash'. The primary meaning of the word that is used here is 'female breast' (it is the word *mastos*, from which we get our word 'mastic', which is how we talk in medical terms about the breast and the mother's milk). Like the word 'breast', it could be used for the male, too – 'chest' is perhaps less committed to male or female – but still, primarily and generally, it means the female.

Of course, we must remember that we are talking about models here – pictures painted, with depths of meaning linking ancient prophecy to its fulfilment in the book of Revelation with the resurrected Christ (see also Luke 20:35). We are not talking about whether Jesus is literally male or female – here on earth He was male. This is hardly surprising, is it? The presentation of Wisdom here, within the work of the Son of Man, comes over to us in the form of a woman, just as it does in Proverbs. So the Arians were not too wrong to identify Wisdom in Proverbs chapter 8 with the Son of God. They seem to have had pretty good biblical grounds for that identification, as did the writer to the Hebrews in 1:2, '. . . through whom also He made the world', which reflects Proverbs 8:30–1.

So, on to the Arian question: does Proverbs 8:22 mean that Jesus *had a beginning*, that he was in fact created, as the Arians maintained?

> The Lord possessed me at the beginning of His way,
> before His works of old.

This was really the proof text for the Arians, so let us examine it more closely. Some versions have translated this verse as, 'The Lord *created* me at the beginning of his work, the first of His acts of old' (rsv), or as, 'Yahweh *created* me, first-fruits of His fashioning, before the oldest of His works' (njb). This is obviously the sense in which Arius understood it in his day, as do the Jehovah's Witnesses in ours. However, the word used is not the usual word for 'create' – it is, rather, the word 'possessed', the same word that is used when Melchizedek says:

> Blessed be Abram of the Most High God, *Possessor* of
> Heaven and Earth. (Genesis 14:19)

Now, of course, if you create something, you own it; nonetheless, creating and owning are not exactly the same concept, which is why some have confused them. Thus, as the Arians said, 'here Wisdom was created', we would say, no, Wisdom is conceived, or begotten, as the eternal begetting of the Son of God.

God is conceiving His thought, His Word, all the time. God's Word coexists with God Himself. His thinking is there all the time. His Wisdom is there all the time. This is what the Cappadocian fathers, and Origen before them, came to call the 'eternal generation of the Son of God'. Whereas the Father was ingenerate – God's thought has always been there – His Word, His *logos*, His logic, is all the time being generated within the Godhead. And that is how Jesus is the revealer of God to us – He is the generating of God which can then be seen, just as the word first appears in the mind and then we speak it. So the second person of the Trinity (as we sometimes refer to Him) communicates God's eternal thinking to us.

As for 'He owned me, possessed me, at the beginning of His way' – what was the beginning of God's way? When did God begin? Whenever He began, Wisdom began. Whenever God began, the Word began. 'At the beginning of His way' is clearly a lovely poetic way of talking about God's eternity. So the Wisdom of God, or the Word of God, was not created at a certain point in time but has always been the eternal possession of an eternal God. God has been eternally thinking, has been eternally generating His Wisdom. Furthermore, it goes on to say in the second half of the verse, 'The LORD possessed me at the beginning of His way, *before His works of old.*' So we cannot (as the Arians tried to do) say that 'at the beginning of His way' means 'when He started to create'. Rather, it is quite the reverse. 'Before His works of old' makes it clear that Wisdom was there before the Lord started the work of creation.

So the Arians were not right in this; and nor, therefore, are the Jehovah's Witnesses today. This was their one great foundation from which they argued, and it is really one of the only places you can go to try and argue that the Son of God is a created being, as opposed to the eternally generated Word or Wisdom or Son of God.

It is perhaps worth looking, at this point, at one or two other potential misunderstandings that may arise in connection with this passage in Proverbs. Verse 25 states, 'Before mountains were settled, before the hills I was brought forth', and we find the same phrase in verse 24: 'I was brought forth'. Some have translated this as 'I was born', but, again, this communicates the idea of begetting. As we have said, Origen introduced the phrase 'the eternal begetting of the Son of God' at the beginning of the third century. And as we have just seen, it is a process that is going on all the time, just like our thinking is being begotten all the time. The focus of the passage then moves on to show Wisdom's relationship to the earth. That is why the phrase comes in at this point – *before the hills were brought forth, I have a relationship to the universe; I was already possessed at the beginning of God's way.* God owns His thinking about creation before He created.

Even if one allowed that you could translate 'possessed' as 'create' (and it would be an inadequate translation), it would still be a very poor way of trying to demonstrate the beginning of the Son of God. Take the philosophical side of the argument for a moment – how can God be an eternal Father if He doesn't have an eternal Son? If there was a certain point in time when the Son was created, then there would have been a time before that point when God was not a Father. However, Jesus reflects the eternal Fatherhood of God when He is called the 'Eternal Father' in Isaiah 9. It is not that He is the same person as the Father, but that, by being the Son, He expresses the eternal Fatherhood of God. 'He who has seen Me, has seen the Father', He says (John 14:9).

### The nature of Jesus

We turn now to look at a wonderful aspect of the nature of our Lord which comes out of these verses in Proverbs, and especially as we connect them with Psalm 2 – a Psalm which tells of the Messiah who was to come. For Jesus was three times 'begotten', three times 'Christ-ed' and three times 'Son of God' (or was 'Son of God' in three ways). To show you what I mean we will turn to Psalm 2 first, and then go back and connect it with our passage in Proverbs.

### *Three 'begettings'*

In Psalm 2:7 the Messiah declares:

> I will surely tell of the decree of the LORD:
> He said to Me, 'You are My Son,
> Today I have begotten You.'

It is a pity, but at this point we need to clear up a bit of confusion. In this verse (and this, unfortunately, is not the only place), the NIV has added in a word that is not there in the Hebrew text of the Bible. While the NIV is to be commended for being a very readable version, this unfortunate habit of going beyond translation into the less steady waters of interpretation makes it sometimes a rather misleading tool for study. Thus it interprets this verse as, 'You are my Son; today I have become Your Father'. Now, ordinary people like me would, naturally, expect the word 'Father' (or something related to it) to be there in the Hebrew text. Let me assure you, that is not the case. The word 'Father' is absent. The way it has been translated makes it appear that Jesus only became God's Son at the resurrection. Quite clearly, this is not what the Bible says. This is all a great shame, because this is such a wonderful verse! It says, 'You are My Son, today I have begotten You'. The word 'Son' is there – the Son of God. And it does not say 'today I have become Your Father', but rather 'today I have begotten You'.

And now we can talk about the three 'begettings'. Jesus, the Son of God, is *eternally* being begotten. He has a second begetting when he was conceived in the womb of Mary and was begotten (you might say) *of the Holy Spirit*. And He has a third begetting when He is *raised from the dead* (Psalm 2:7). In Acts 2:24, in the Greek, it says God 'put an end to the birth-pangs of death' (now that is an interesting phrase, isn't it?), and He bursts out of the grave in resurrection. He is raised from the dead and is born out of Hades. He is born out of the grave into the life that we will share with Him.

You see, we do not share eternal life (in the strictest sense of the term) with Jesus because, unlike Him, we do not go back into eternity. Nor do we get involved at all – or share with Him – in the incarnate birth from Mary. We were not virgin born, although we can make an analogy with being born again. But we do completely share with Him the third begetting, when He was raised from the dead and 'declared the Son of God with power by the resurrection from the dead' (Romans 1:4). And as He leads 'many sons to glory' (Hebrews 2:10), and is the 'first fruits' of those who will be raised from death (1 Corinthians 15:20), we will share completely with Him! We shall be begotten in resurrection!

We can further see this connection between 'today I have begotten You' and the resurrection of Jesus when we look at the verse before where God says, 'But as for Me, I have installed My King upon Zion, My holy mountain' (v6). Here is the installation of Jesus, through resurrection and then ascension, into the place of kingship, rule and authority.

### *Three 'Christ-ings'*
This idea brings us straight back to our passage in Proverbs 8, and to verses 22–3, where the Messiah says:

> The LORD possessed me at the beginning of His way, before His works of old. From everlasting I was *established*.

84

This is the same word we have just seen in Psalm 2:6 – Jesus was 'installed', or 'established' – but here (in Proverbs 8) it is from all eternity. The word 'installed' (Hebrew *nacak*) can also be translated 'anointed', from its primary meaning 'to pour out'. So now we have three 'anointings' or 'Christ-ings' ('Christ' means 'anointed One').

So what, then, is this 'installing', or 'establishing', or 'Christ-ing', *'from everlasting'* (v23)? It is, I believe, where the Lord was living in a position of authority and of the Christ before He ever came to earth. For eternity Jesus has had an 'anointing'; for eternity He has been 'Christ-ed'. That is why, when He was born here on earth, it does not say, 'for today in the city of David there has been born for you a Saviour, who *will become* Christ the Lord', but rather 'who *is* Christ the Lord' (see Luke 2:11). He has existed eternally in this position of being the Anointed One. He has eternally held this function within the Godhead. And now He comes to earth, and it is recognized that He is *already* the Christ!

Second, at His baptism the Holy Spirit comes upon Him. The Father says, 'This is My beloved Son, in Whom I am well pleased.' John the Baptist notes that the Holy Spirit *'remained* upon Him', which is how John knew that He was the Messiah, the One that would come after him (John 1:32–4). This, therefore, is the second 'Christ-ing', or anointing, that Jesus had – when He was here on earth. Peter refers to this in Acts 10:38:

> Jesus of Nazareth, how God anointed Him with the Holy Spirit and with power, and how He went about doing good and healing all who were oppressed by the devil, for God was with Him.

Third, having risen again, He ascends to heaven and He is

'installed . . . upon Zion, My holy mountain' (as we just saw, in Psalm 2:6). He is 'installed' or, again, 'anointed', 'Christ-ed'. Then, in the first chapter of Hebrews it says that, having

> made purification of sins, He sat down at the right hand
> of the Majesty on high . . . [and was] 'anointed . . . with
> the oil of gladness above [His] companions'.

And then He pours out this Spirit. He received the Spirit; He was anointed with the Spirit; and 'poured forth this which you both see and hear' (Acts 2:33). So, once again, just as with the 'begettings', we can share with Him in this third aspect of His 'Christ-ing'.

### *Three times 'Son of God'*
So Jesus was three times 'begotten', three times 'Christ-ed' and, you could say, three times 'Son of God'. First, He is the eternal Son of the Father.

Second, when He was born of Mary, He was the Son of God by the generation of the Spirit into the womb of Mary. It was partly because of this 'Son-of-God-ness' that Mary could not even try to save her son, and so Jesus died; for Mary could not deny the virgin birth, nor that it was not Joseph, but God who was His Father. Thus Jesus died on the charge, 'He was the Son of God'. She would have done anything to save her son, saying, *He's out of his mind – of course he is not the Son of God; I was there at the time, and so was Joseph.* That was the one thing that might have saved Jesus from the cross. Any mother would have pleaded it, but Mary couldn't. She knew what had happened. She knew that He was conceived by the Holy Spirit. This second 'Son-of-God-ness' also takes up the concept of Jesus being God's servant here on earth – as Israel was called by God 'My son' (Exodus 4:22). Israel fails in sonship, but God says 'this is My Son' and points to

Jesus (Matthew 3:17). That is why Matthew 2:15 refers to Hosea 11:1, and to Jesus fulfilling this prophecy.

Third, as we saw, He is:

> declared the Son of God with power by the resurrection
> from the dead. (Romans 1:4)

And as He rises from the grave, and calls many sons to glory, a new family has come into being – of which He invites us to be a part! He is the 'elder brother' and, being the firstborn from the dead, He is to be also 'the firstborn of many brothers'! So Jesus is Son of God by resurrection, in which we shall share.

## Judaism

Judaism is another tradition that opposes the idea of the Trinity; and, being a monotheistic religion, it says that God is One alone. The idea that anyone could be made equal with God or share His glory was, and is, anathema. Of course, this is just what we see happening in John 5:17–23. Jesus says, 'My Father is working until now, and I Myself am working.' And He goes on to say that He always does what the Father is doing. The result is (v18):

> For this cause therefore the Jews were seeking all the
> more to kill Him, because He not only was breaking the
> Sabbath, but also was calling God His own Father.

What did all of this mean to the Jews of Jesus' day? Jesus was calling God His 'own Father' and justifying His actions by saying He was doing what the Father was doing. He was 'making Himself equal with God', as they said of Him at the end of verse 18, and this is what they found most objectionable about Jesus. His assertions made Him equal to God, and there can only be one God.

At this point, we should also note something else that comes out of this John 5 passage, regarding the theme of subordination and equality that we have already met in chapter four. Jesus says:

> Truly, truly, I say to you, the Son can do nothing of Himself, unless it is something He sees the Father doing; for whatever the Father does, these things the Son also does in like manner. For the Father loves the Son, and shows Him all things that He Himself is doing; and the Father will show Him greater works than these, so that you will marvel. For just as the Father raises the dead and gives them life, even so the Son also gives life to whom He wishes. For not even the Father judges anyone, but He has given all judgment to the Son. (v19–22)

The Father here is seen as the source within the Godhead. He is the one that the Son looks to before He does anything. But the Father isn't going to judge! He is going to give all judgement to the Son. In the same way, the Father could be the one who raises the dead to life in the final resurrection, but He has delegated this task to His Son (as the Son is the one who was incarnate and was to experience resurrection). And then, in the next verse, Jesus goes on to say:

> [The Father . . . has given all judgment to the Son] so that all will honour the Son, even as they honour the Father. He who does not honour the Son does not honour the Father who sent Him. (v23)

The wonderful thing is that the Son is always honouring the Father, and now the Father is saying that He wants us to honour the Son, just as we honour Him. There is a constant giving away of honour, a constant giving place to one another, in the Trinity.

In Mark 10:45 we see Jesus saying that He will be the suffering servant, and that He will die – even the death of the cross (see also Philippians 2). He will make himself of no reputation and will not hold on to existing in the same manner as God. But then the Father takes Him and lifts Him up and says that He wants everybody to acknowledge that Jesus is Lord. The Father gives Him the name which is above every name, that at the name of Jesus every knee shall bow and every tongue confess He is Lord.

So the Father and the Son are equals – equals in meaning, in capacity, in life, and so on. But while the Son is always making Himself subordinate to the Father, the Father is always counteracting His Son's subordination in wanting the Son to receive the honour and be glorified (of course, I am not referring here to subordinationism, which was a fourth-century heresy rejected by the Church).

This humility, this giving away of glory, exists within the Godhead. If it didn't, the 'god' we would be worshipping would be an isolated, arrogant god. Some people complain about giving God glory, saying, 'Why on earth should we glorify Him? What is He like, that He wants so much glory?' But it is within the Godhead that glory is being given, one to another – back and forth. (And anyway, it is the best thing for us, to give Him glory. It is only when we see something bigger and more wonderful than ourselves that some of our arrogance gets removed.)

## The Muslims

We mentioned earlier the fact that Islam has three eternals: the eternal God, Allah; the eternal Koran; and the eternal spirit of Allah. Philosophically, you cannot have three eternal things coexisting independently without their being coequal. In other words, one is driven to accept either Tri-theism (belief in three gods), or else a Trinity – if there is to be only one God. The eternal Koran, the eternal Spirit and the eternal Allah somehow need to be brought into one. The Muslims, of course, do not acknowledge that they need a trinity, nor do they want to say that they worship three gods; they are vehemently monotheistic. But, nevertheless, they are stuck with three eternals. They do not like the idea, but they should be as equally Trinitarian as we are. They have a problem, though, in the fact that one of their eternals is a book, rather than a person.

Muslims have also put over a caricature of our concept of the Trinity by saying that we worship the Father, the Son and Mary; and this is one of the things in our conversations with them that we need to put right. Since there are millions of Muslims all over the world, we will find that we are going to have to talk about the Trinity often. There are some Christians and converts from Islam who, while believing in the Trinity themselves, find it difficult to expect Muslims to understand the doctrine. Nonetheless, we still need to be able to explain ourselves in a way that they can grasp; and also in a way that stimulates worship, because you worship your way into the heart of God. Our enjoyment, wonder and reasoned acceptance of the Trinitarian God, therefore, can become an important vehicle for leading a Muslim to Christ.

### New Age spirituality

The reason I have included believers in the New Age is because of the new 'spirituality' that exists in sections of our culture today, where Jesus is regarded as just one helpful guide among others, someone who carried a certain amount of truth. He is seen as a guru, a master of disciplines and of teaching. New Age adherents frequently put Jesus alongside their collection of other great teachers, so that disciples and teachers – including

Jesus – are all seekers together. We need, therefore, to be able to communicate to such people the uniqueness of God the Father, Son and Spirit. We need to show how our use of the word 'God' means something very different from their use of the word (with, we would say, a small 'g').

God is unknown in character and person, unless He reveals Himself to us, which we assert He has done in Jesus. Our view of Jesus will appear to those who adhere to postmodern spirituality as one among many speculations. We can at least use this openness to spirituality in general to gain a hearing and communicate our understanding of Jesus as a revelation from God. Christians can also give those lost in a sea of various spiritualities a metanarrative – a structure which makes sense of the universe, of our deepest needs and longings for love and significance.

## Oneness Pentecostals

A movement called the 'Oneness Movement' is growing in the United States. While they are not nearly as big as the Pentecostal movement, they have split from the 'orthodox' Pentecostals and call themselves the 'Oneness Pentecostals'. They are also known as the 'Jesus Only' movement, the 'Apostolic Pentecostals' or simply as 'those who baptize in the name of Jesus'. They hold the unorthodox view that baptism *must* be done in the name of Jesus, rather than in the name of the Father, the Son and the Holy Spirit. They believe that the Trinitarian formula (see Matthew 28:19) is not valid, and that it was slipped in later on in church history. They maintain that all of the Early Church fathers who talked about the Trinity got it wrong. It is rather an ambitious claim to assert that they alone, in the course of two thousand years, have recovered the original meaning of Jesus in the Gospels!

The Oneness view is popular, nonetheless, because it is easily assimilated – it fits well with the way we often operate on a practical level. I am sure you have heard Christians in prayer meetings who say, 'Dear Father, Son, Holy Spirit, Lord . . .' and get all the names and titles mixed up as they pray. Well, the Oneness Pentecostals have a very simple solution to all of this apparent confusion. They say that the Father = the Son = the Spirit – and that it is all in Jesus. They believe that the Father and Jesus are, in fact, the same person, and that the Spirit is not a person at all, but either a manifestation of Jesus' power or a synonym for Him.

To give the scriptural basis for what they are doing, the Oneness Pentecostals go to the Acts of the Apostles and point to the cases where people are, or talk about being, baptized upon, or in, the name of Jesus. Hence they say that they, too, should baptize *in the name of* Jesus. But the fact of the matter is that when you baptize in the name of someone, it is just the same sort of thing as saying, 'open up *in the name of* the Queen'. In other words, they were doing so on Jesus' authority. And the authority of Jesus was that (if you want a formula) we baptize in the name of the Father, the Son and the Holy Spirit (Matthew 28:19). I'm not sure how important the formula is in general to Jesus, but every time we use it, we are asserting something fundamental about our faith. On the authority of Jesus, therefore, we baptize with the Trinitarian formula – because it was Jesus who gave us the authority to do so.

## Liberals

Finally, we come in our list of opponents of the doctrine of the Trinity to the liberal theologians. Some years ago at Easter, the BBC showed a programme about Jesus called *The Evidence* (which really turned out to be the 'lack of evidence', unfortunately).

I had the privilege of debating with the producer. What he was attempting to do was to put across the idea that Jesus was originally just a simple teacher who said great things such as, 'Love your neighbour' and 'Love God'. Later on, by the fourth century, this had all become much more complicated, he said. Jesus had now become a God, and had been elevated into the Godhead (much the same as the argument we saw under the section on sceptics, above). What we needed to do now, he argued, was to get back to Jesus the simple Galilean peasant, stripping away all the complicated stuff about him being God and that necessitating a Trinity.

This argument is often taken up by liberal theologians who desire, as they would put it, to 'clean up and make simple' our Christianity. Men such as Rauschenbusch in the United States and others on both sides of the Atlantic have tried to downplay the theology of the atonement and the Trinity. They want to say that Christianity loses nothing by getting rid of these things. It is really very simple, they say, and all it actually boils down to is obeying the Sermon on the Mount. Unnecessarily complicated ideas and extra paraphernalia such as the Trinity are just later additions in Church history.

Now, of course, this will not do. We saw earlier (again, in the section on Sceptics) that it is completely inaccurate to say that the Early Church did not have a concept of the Trinity. We have seen the evidence for a belief in the Trinity from long before the fourth century.

The liberals have also complained that Greek philosophy is responsible for making the 'simple truths of Jesus' into the 'complicated doctrines of the Church'. However, even when we go back to the original Hebrew ideas of Jesus' day, we are still grappling with rabbinic thought and concepts which are much more subtle and deeper than many liberals would care to allow. These are the kinds of things that the early Greek theologians had to grapple with to come out with such concepts as the generating of the Son of God, the ingenerate Father and the procession of the Holy Spirit.

There *is* something attractive, however, about the idea of simply 'loving God and loving your neighbour'. Of course there is – it is only right! One of the reasons for studying the Trinity is *because* we love God, and we want to love Him more. Isn't that the reason why we study one another? A husband who never studies his wife and has brought her a cup of tea every morning for the last thirty years, when she has been saying that she doesn't like tea and prefers coffee, is hardly said to be a great lover! We want to know more of God and more of His glory. We want to love Him more deeply as we grow in the knowledge of who He is and the wonders of His love.

It is the aim of theological debate and interest to get deeper into an understanding of our God, and at the same time, too, it is a wonderful thing to remember that there is always going to be a mystery about this. I am not overly fond of Augustine, but he did say at one time that if we understand it, then it is not God. What he meant, of course, was not that we cannot have a revelation of God (and that revelation, if it means what it says – if it is *revelation* – to some degree has to be understandable), but he is saying virtually that the God who made such a complex universe as this cannot possibly be exhausted by even the deepest enquiries that our human minds can make. There will always be something more. There will always be more in that iceberg than we can ever actually take in ourselves, whether we are on a level looking at the top of the iceberg, or whether we are looking down from above at the bigger part of it beneath the sea; there is always more about God to try to know. And that is what causes some of the difficulties of dealing with this subject – and, always, leaves plenty of room for more worship.

# 7

# Practical Relevance of the Trinity

There are some, even among Christians, who may suggest or think that the doctrine of the Trinity is not really very practical. As we have seen in chapter six, however, we need to understand the Trinity when we are debating with, or trying to understand, the opponents of Christianity. And that is just one aspect of the Trinity's practical relevance for us in the Church today. We will look now at some further reasons why we should study this wonderful truth about our God, and how it impacts the thoughts we think and the way we live. There are eight areas in which I believe this current enquiry into the subject of the Trinity has some practical significance.

## 1. Unity movement (ecumenism)

Most of us will be aware that once again there has been, of late, a strong recognition that the Church should be at one. We need, somehow, to stand together. But there is much current debate as to how this unity should express itself. Should it be an external, bureaucratic unity? Or perhaps a political sort of unity? Some wish for a unity that is on paper – in which we agree on certain things and agree to disagree on others. Most would agree that this unity has to be visible, but you can't necessarily *see* a unity that is written down on a piece of paper. Before we attempt to answer this question, let us first ask another question. Where does this current desire for church unity come from?

The great boost forward in church unity came, I would suggest, with the Moravian movement in the eighteenth century. This was really the beginning of the ecumenical movement. The Moravians were the first to bring together successfully all sorts of denominations and disparate groups, and were the first to maintain that unity was an important aspect in world evangelization. Jesus had prayed:

> that they may all be one; even as You, Father, are in Me, and I in You, that they also may be in Us; *so that the world may believe* that You sent Me. (John 17:21)

And again,

> that they may be one, just as We are one; I in them, and You in Me, that they may be perfected in unity, *so that the world may know* that You sent Me, and loved them, even as You have loved Me. (John 17:22–3)

Church unity and the task of evangelizing the world are bound up together.

Out of this great missionary movement (for the Moravians travelled the earth, telling people the good news of Jesus), the ecumenical movement was birthed. The Methodists, after them, also emphasized this unity. They were in a sense connected to the Moravians because of John Wesley's conversion through the Moravian Peter Boehler. The Methodists maintained that it was a unity of love, and therefore anyone who loved Christ sincerely was welcomed at the Lord's table. This sort of thing was revolutionary; it had never been done before.

Then in the nineteenth century – the great missionary century – the attempt to evangelize the world became the great Protestant theme, and missions began to spring up and move out into all the world. (Of course, it should be noted that the Catholics had already been at this task from the mid-fifteenth to the mid-seventeenth centuries, and now the Protestants caught on too). This great missionary effort gave us a common goal – to try to reach the ends of the earth with the gospel. This kind of ecumenism was based on the idea that *we have got to do this together; it is too big a task for one group of believers to achieve alone.* And so this, in turn, added to the growing desire for church unity.

Now we come to our present time, to the twentieth and twenty-first centuries. I suggested in the introduction that there are three 'levels' of unity, if you like, based on the three persons of the Trinity. We have seen these 'levels' worked out in church history (see chapter four), and now we will see how they might be applied to the last century and into our current time.

### *The unity of the Spirit (common believing)*
With the charismatic movement spreading throughout the historic churches in the mid-twentieth century came a great advance in church unity. It was inevitable that the hearts of people in different denominations would be opened up to one another, because it was the same Holy Spirit who was working in all. As a result, we saw that our commonality was not only in attempts to agree a common creed. Nor was it simply in the fact that we all carried the same name – Christian. Our commonality was that we had the same Holy Spirit, and this brought about a terrific change. Up until then, for example, the Catholic Church had been almost impregnable to any inroads of ecumenism. They had not fully participated in the 1910 missionary conference in Edinburgh and stood, really, on the

touchlines. But when the charismatic movement began, just prior to Vatican II and all of the changes that began to take place, this unity of the Spirit began to be experienced in Catholic areas, too. Even if not everybody engaged, there was still a fundamental change in the attitude towards other movements and denominations.

This growing desire for unity is only to be expected, of course, as it is the Holy Spirit's presence that enables us to think and to understand the truths of God. He takes the things of Christ and shows them to us (John 16:13–4). As He illuminates our hearts and enables us to see Jesus, we have a commonality in the Holy Spirit as we begin to think and to believe similarly.

## *Christological unity (common behaviour)*
The story does not stop there, however. Belief leads to behaviour, and our second level is what we might call christological unity. As the Spirit moves in our hearts, so the people we meet across the various denominations touch our hearts because of what we see of Jesus in them. In this way, Jesus starts to become the centre of our ecumenical thinking. We now have a common understanding (and much more common than it was) of the person of Jesus. The commonality of the unity of the Spirit makes us begin to *think* the same way; the revelation of Jesus begins to challenge us to behave in a Jesus way. And the more we *behave* in a Jesus way, the more we sense, and feel, that we are one.

There is a man from the papal court who regularly preaches to the Pope, whom I went to hear not so long ago (for the second time). I went just to listen to this man talk about Jesus, and to touch his life. You know when you are touching the same things of Jesus that you are aware of yourself. It is the same Jesus. The tragedy was that he still could not break bread with us because of his tradition. But his love of Christ and his behaviour we could understand together. On the other hand, I do not understand the behaviour of a man who claims to be a Christian but who is willing to burn other people at the stake (as some famous people in church history have done). It may be argued that such was the spirit of the age, but if so then these men were of the spirit of the age, and it has nothing to do with the Spirit of God. I have never been able to understand how it is that the behaviour of those who say that they are following Jesus can be so contradictory to His lifestyle.

This next stage of unity that we have been experiencing has, I believe, been the way in which Christians are now demonstrating Christ, more and more, in the things that they do. Belief leads to behaviour.

### Unity in the Father (common belonging)

I want to suggest that there is a third stage of unity yet to come. Perhaps it is already beginning. It is a unity that stems not only from the Spirit and from our common belief. It is a unity not only with Jesus, that means we can begin to behave in a Christlike manner. It is a unity that comes about with the sense of belonging to the same Father, with the sense that we are one family.

Now, of course, when we are one family, there are fewer barriers to breaking bread together, because we are eating as sons and daughters of the King, around the Father's table. We are living on His provision, recognizing that our identity is found in the fact that we belong to the same family. And we will become more and more aware of the diversity that exists within the unity.

So the Trinity helps us to understand our common believing, behaving and belonging. When we get to the stage where the barriers are broken down, and we feast together in the Father's house, then we will also have the unity that is in relationship to God the Father, here on earth now, and in the New Jerusalem for ever.

## 2. Body life (church)

As distinct from church unity across various denominations, I want now to look at 'body life'. This is the unity that is found within the body of Christ as each part of the body, each person, contributes towards the building up of the one body. Body life is a term that is very common today; when I was a young Christian, it was not. It means that, in some way or other, we live and share together. Then, on the basis of the cross, which cuts out the flesh, we begin to learn to live and to make room for one another; we begin to express more of the totality of what it means to be in the body of Christ.

This concept of body life is also important for those of us (both in traditional denominations and in the newer churches) who want to emphasize the importance of being a non-clerical church. Of course we believe in leaders and in leadership, but we also believe in a community of people who are living together as part of a body, and who are thus contributing to one another. We are seeing this emphasis throughout the Church of Christ. More and more, we are realizing that those of us who lead do not belong to some special, elitist class that is seeking to serve in the things of God. We belong to a total community of people who share a common life, each seeking to serve and bless one another. Body life is community; it is fellowship; it is relationship. Even the physical layouts of church buildings are changing so that, instead of staring at the back of somebody's neck all the time, you can now look into each other's faces. What does this mean? It means that the Spirit of God has been emphasizing relationships. Why? Because God *is* a bunch of relationships.

Body life is not about a few people at the front doing everything. It is, rather, a reflection, or an outworking, of the fact that God is not 'up front', doing a kind of play-acting for us to watch and be entertained and not really participate in. Incidentally, on this note we also need to counter the celebrity spirit of the twenty-first century. We are, instead, looking around, sharing and caring. We are saying that we are all important in this community, and we are learning how to have a common life together.

The more we emphasize the Trinitarian God, the more it all makes sense, and the more likely it is that all of these things will take place. The Trinity consists of three equal entities within one entity who are sharing together and living with and making room for one another; who are giving way to one another, subordinating themselves to one another. They do all of this in order that the glory and the wonder of life in God can be expressed and be made known in and through the body life of human beings in the Church. If we have a relational God, we have relational churches.

The Eastern Church, on the one hand, has always laid greater emphasis on what is known as the 'social Trinity', the interaction of equal persons within the relationship of the Godhead. On the other hand, the Western Church (and therefore most of Protestantism) has inherited the tradition of the 'psychological Trinity', where we try to find different centres of awareness within one person. The social Trinity emphasizes the distinct persons, and therefore the relationships, within the Godhead; the psychological Trinity concentrates on the 'oneness', at the expense of the 'threeness' and the relationships. It is not that one is wrong and the other is right, it is rather that they are different analogies trying to express the Trinitarian God, and we have to hold the two together. But it is worth bearing in mind that relational churches will develop where there is a strong emphasis on the distinct persons and their relationships within the Trinity – you become like the thing you worship. Emphasizing the social Trinity will increase our longing for unity, though both models contribute to our understanding of the Godhead.

It is also worth noting that there is really no sense of hierarchy in the understanding of the social Trinity. If, as in the Western world, we have God the Father, the first person of the Trinity; God the Son, the second person of the Trinity; and God the Holy Spirit, the third person of the Trinity, then we have a hierarchy: one, two, three. If, on the other hand, we emphasize the social Trinity – as in the Eastern Church – we have God the Father; God-out-of-God, the Son; and God-out-of-God, the Holy Spirit. And you cannot really say that there is a hierarchy when there is a source and two expressions, or, as Irenaeus would put it, when there is a body and two hands.

The more we become aware of the relational aspect of the Trinity, the relationships between the Three-in-One, the more we will see the importance of a relational church.

### 3. Rediscovering the masculine and feminine

There has been a great concern among many Christians, including theologians, in the twentieth and twenty-first centuries to rediscover the feminine within God. Of course (as we have said), what we are referring to is the feminine, not the female, for God is beyond gender. In the history of the world and – to our shame – in the Church, too, the feminine has often been put down; women have had no place and have often been made out to be some kind of substandard human beings. Hence, of late, there has been a resurgence of the awareness of the feminine within God. The image of the Spirit as a gentle dove, the fact that 'Spirit' (*ruach*) is grammatically feminine in the Hebrew, are just two of the different ways in which we can begin to say that the feminine is equally there within the Godhead. We also noted in chapter six that the figure of Wisdom, whom the New Testament picks up on as being Jesus, is female. The image of the triple helix from chapter five also helps us to see this aspect of God more clearly. The derivation of woman from man is related to that of the proceeding of the Spirit from God, and the generation of the child from a man to that of the Son (the message) being begotten of God. This image perhaps introduces something of the 'mother' aspect of the feminine into the Godhead, and so into our understanding of the Trinity. We need, of course, to be careful. For it is one thing to say, 'God is *like* a mother in some respects, as He is *like* a father in others'; but to say, 'God is Mother' would be to move away from the biblical revelation.

When we see that the Son of God and the Spirit of God are equal with the Father in all respects, and yet give way to one another, we begin to understand how the aspect of service and subordination is contained within the Godhead. There is a genuine diversity within the unity of God, in which is found all the mutuality, all the reciprocity of cooperation and of unity and peace, in the ways in which these relationships work together. Is this not what the feminine brings into our community and society, in contrast to macho aggression? There is a need to discover these elements afresh, not just in one person of the Godhead (for example, the Spirit), but in the way that the members of the Godhead relate to one another. They are neither male nor female, but they are masculine and feminine equally. In this way we can genuinely understand the feminine within God, which is necessary if we are to recapture the masses of the feminist movement who have sincerely approached a Christianity that has only given place to the feminine in the worship of Mary (who has been elevated almost to membership within the Godhead itself). The Trinitarian God, whose three persons are constantly giving way and making room for each other within the mutuality of the Godhead, allows for this rediscovery.

## 4. The pre-eminence of love

We believe that love is the pre-eminent value in the universe; and therefore, as such, it must be found in God. We noted in the introduction that, incredible though it may seem, no Christian creed has ever asserted a description of God as Love – in spite of the fact that 'God is love' (1 John 4:7–19) is one of the unique and fundamental assertions of Christianity.

We have seen that Love cannot exist in itself. It must have an object. Self-love is, in a sense, a perversion. Therefore, God could only have become loving when He created something to love – the universe – unless, of course, love somehow exists permanently within God. If love does not exist permanently within God, then love is not pre-eminent and it is not the first value in the universe – something else is.

And, of course, many Christians believe that something else is pre-eminent. In certain quarters you have only to say, 'God is Love', and, 'the love of God has given His only Son', and you will find someone saying, 'Thank you very much; but he is also . . .' Many people try to qualify the love. But the love, in fact, qualifies everything else. God is a judge, but He is a loving judge; God is a redeemer, but He is a loving redeemer; God is a Father, but He is a loving Father, and so on. Love is the prime value that determines everything else that we assert about God. It is the great characteristic of the persons of the Godhead. It exists among the members of the Trinity and, if there were no multiplicity within the unity, then love could not exist at all.

In order to be able to assert that the primary thing is *God is love*, that He has always been that and always will be, we need a Trinitarian God; a God who is a bunch of relationships and is, therefore, eternally loving. He really is love, in Himself; the Father, the Son and the Holy Spirit have always been giving way, and loving, and sharing, and in relationship, before ever there was a creation. And now that love is spilling over into the world, into the universe.

The emphasis on a loving God, and our holding on to this first of all values, can only come about from a Trinitarian understanding of God. The idea that God exists in the sole aloneness of himself, with no plurality, is chaotic and meaningless. Such a concept merely leads us to a kind of unattractive and empty oblivion. But the truth that God exists in three relational entities held in one opens the door for love to exist before the world began.

## 5. The challenge to evangelize in contemporary culture

We will look briefly now at two great dichotomies in the world today to which, I believe, we have an answer in the Trinitarian God of Christianity. The first is the opposing and, in a sense, opposite systems of monotheistic Islam and polytheistic Hinduism. While we have mentioned this before, the Trinitarian concept of a plurality within a unity should provide a clear answer here, as it should appeal to those who have found flaws or inadequacies in either system. We are not polytheists, neither are we strict (deist) monotheists – we are monotheistic Trinitarians!

The second dichotomy I want to touch on is that found in the modern/postmodern debate. The word 'modern' comes from the Latin *modus*, meaning 'now', so to be 'post-now' seems to present something of a problem! Still, the terms refer to two major positions we find in Western culture today, of which the rationalistic basis of the modernists has provided the opportunity for the experiential and deconstructionist position of the postmodernists. Thus, philosophically there is a need for a God who contains something of a mystery and yet can be rationally appreciated. There is a place for revelation, which leads one on into further discovery.

Science is just like that, anyway. In our explorations and investigations, we go from atoms to particles to quantum physics, and then to great mysteries that lie beyond that. Who knows where it shall ever end? The same discovery and enquiry into God will help us to present our case reasonably and rationally to the modernists, and experientially and meaningfully to the postmodernists. We ought also to be able to drive down the middle of this one. We ought to be able to take advantage of the hearing that postmodernism gives us (as it listens to all views), and yet at the same time to explain that we have revelation, and that there is something that can be understood.

## 6. To authenticate the incarnation and atonement

Without the Trinity, the incarnation makes little or no sense at all. We would have the problem of how God could be in heaven and also be addressed in prayer as 'Father' at the same time by God here on earth. There would be the problem of how the universe could still be held together when the infinite God became finite and went to sleep here on earth. With a 'monistic God', these things would be impossible to explain.

If it was Jesus who came and did the work of the atonement, who suffered all the agony and pain of the cross, and I love Him because He did all that for me – *greater love has no one than this, that one lay down his life for his friends* – then where does this leave the distant deist god of, for example, the Jehovah's Witnesses? If Jesus has done all that is necessary; has paid the price; and He loves me and I love Him back, then He is the one whom I can understand and love. Where, therefore, does this other 'god' come into the picture?

> There is . . . one mediator . . . between God and men,
> the man Christ Jesus. (1 Timothy 2:5)

He must be a true mediator who can fully represent both God's interests *and* humankind's. The only one who can do this is a 'Godman'. Thus, our very grasp of the incarnation and atonement depends upon a Trinitarian God.

It is important that we are able to put this across meaningfully and coherently. There is a common misunderstanding that is encapsulated in the story of *Miracle on the River Kwai*, in which a young man from a university in Scotland, having survived the horrors of a Second World War Japanese concentration camp, comes away thinking that Christianity is an angry Father and a loving Son. This is a terrible misunderstanding; it produces a schizophrenic God. We know that Jesus was Himself angry – when the children were turned away from Him; with His disciples, and with the Pharisees; and with the abuse of His Father's house. There is equally anger in the Son of God as in the Father, because one reveals the other: 'He who has seen Me has seen the Father' (John 14:9).

Clearly, the idea of an angry Father and a loving Son would make the atonement into a nonsense. He must be that one and the same God who is involved in the cross. Therefore Paul says, 'God was in Christ reconciling the world to Himself' (2 Corinthians 5:19). The Father was equally involved in the work of reconciliation. Humanity's defection and sin evoked His anger; but it is the same God who is experiencing that anger on the cross and who is thus exhausting His anger *within Himself* and is bringing – out of love – a solution to this dilemma, so that men and women can enter a relationship with God.

## 7. To answer the problem of evil adequately

This leads us on to the problem of the existence of evil in a universe created by a loving God. If we are to have anything to say to people in the twenty-first century, I think one of the things we will have to get hold of is the issue of suffering, the problem of evil. Why do good people suffer? Would it not, at least, be better if only bad people suffered? Surely that would make things a lot plainer, at any rate?

The problem of evil has sometimes been answered inadequately. Dare I suggest that it has been answered in what we might call a 'monist', that is, a non-Trinitarian, way? It has been said that God is meticulously ordaining everything, including every one of the greatest evils ever perpetrated by humankind, and that each is part of a greater plan He is working out. The analogy has been perhaps overused of a tapestry that is messy, tangled and ugly on one side and makes no sense until one day it is turned over, and we see the beauty of the design wherein even all of the evil and dark colours have been woven into a perfect picture, so that everything is seen to have been part of God's plan. Now, I don't believe this is correct; the tapestry is, we might say, wearing thin in the face of the horrendous atrocities committed in the last century, and in our time. We cannot expect the many who have survived massacres, or who have lost everything and everyone they hold dear, to listen to us if all we can say is that it has been, somehow, for a loving and good reason. But that is what results from believing in a god who is sole, alone, with no plurality in its oneness, who is not a Trinity.

However, if we have a Trinitarian God, we have a God who has three wills. Some theologians throughout history have denied this; but we have a God who says, *Father, not My will, but Your will be done.* This is a case where, as we said before, we must not split the economic (functional) Trinity from the ontological. In other words, the God we see in history, in Jesus, reveals what God is really like in His eternal essence. There is always, within God, the will of the Father and the will of the Son. There is also, according to the biblical revelation, the will of the Spirit (1 Corinthians 12:11).

Within the Godhead there are three wills that are continually choosing together. The Son's will was able to have been in opposition to the Father's; otherwise the tears and the pleadings and the words of Jesus in Gethsemane were a mockery, a mere charade. But they were real tears, and they were true words when the Son said to the Father, *Let this cup pass from Me, yet not My will, but Your will be done.* There was the possibility within the Godhead of two wills in conflict – and this is the glory of the victory. It has already been won before Jesus goes to Calvary, in the garden of Gethsemane; and after He has said, *Your will be done*, He marches out with triumph to the cross; He is not dragged there as a victim. He has already won the battle, the battle that His will and the Father's will should coincide. The Spirit was equally involved in the atonement, as Christ offered Himself to God 'through the eternal Spirit' (Hebrews 9:14). All three persons of the Godhead are involved, and each of them is saying, *Your will be done*, choosing each other's will; and so God acts as one. He acts from the unity of a diversity of wills within.

So when God makes the universe, it reflects the possibility of wills that could be in opposition to each other. Thus, although the universe is one, there are many wills acting within it, because it reflects the very being of its Creator. If God were not a Trinity, then the universe He made would have had just one will behind it, and we would not have had all the problems that arise from people saying, *My will be done.* That is why there is the problem

111

of evil, and why there is suffering. This does not mean that evil originates from God, but the possibility of evil exists in creation because God is a Trinity and has made us in His image: with wills. The wills in the universe are not coming together as they should, coherently, continuously, dynamically, *Your will be done, Your will be done . . .* We are all trying to get our own will done; and out of that – through the angelic realm, through the human realm, through the multiplicity of all the single individual beings – there are wheels in conflict, until the great peace of God can draw them all together because of what Jesus has done.

(For more on the subject of evil and suffering, please see my book *Suffering and the Love of God: The book of Job*.)

## 8. The basis for the 'servanthood of equals'

While we have looked at this 'subordination of equals' in some detail in chapter four (and also in chapter six, under Judaism), we touch on it again here because it also belongs in this list of ways that the doctrine of the Trinity affects us today. The word 'subordination' in some theologies is a derogatory term, and in others it refers to something very beautiful about the subordination of the Son and the Spirit to the Father. As we have said, we are not talking about the fourth-century heresy of subordinationism, but rather about the mutual giving way to one another, and giving place to one another, the *Your will be done*, that is at work between the Father, the Son and the Holy Spirit. If that is what is happening within the Godhead, if that is the sort of God we worship, then we should become like Him, loving and serving one another in humility.

If our God were not like that, if He were a monarchical packet of power living in sole, unique oneness, then we could only expect to be in relationship with Him as slaves to an overlord. And perhaps, further, it should follow that we should force others to obey this 'overlord', too. But, fortunately, our God is not like that at all. He is a plurality within a unity; He is three who are loving and giving and serving and giving place to one another throughout all eternity, and so when He creates the universe, we (and all creation) are meant to become part of this wondrous dance.

# 8

# Analogies

This chapter contains sixteen analogies – interesting, provocative, profound and fun – to help us reflect on the Trinity. I apologize in advance for my homespun etymology.

*Mathematical analogy*
We have already encountered the mathematical analogy, in chapter six. The fact that we can express a Trinity in mathematics ($1 \times 1 \times 1 = 1$) demonstrates that it is a rational concept, even if it is difficult to imagine in terms of heads and feet. Three units in a relationship of multiplication (a more complex and deeper relationship than simple addition) are still one – so also is the Godhead.

*Dimensional analogy*
God is multi- or even infinitely dimensional, and we are three-dimensional ($1 \times 1 \times 1$ can be expressed another way: $1^3$, ie a perfect cube with a dimension of 1 and a volume of 1). With multiplication, or division, of 1, we just can't get away from 1 – try it! To help us picture this, let us reduce it down to God in three dimensions and ourselves in two, so that we are still keeping the idea of God having more dimensions than we do. A three-dimensional God revealed in a two-dimensional world would be like a sphere moving into a piece of paper – all you see is a circle

as the sphere passes through the paper. We, living in the flat, two-dimensional world of the paper, could never see the sphere as such. We would only see the God-circle – a human being – Jesus. No human being has seen the sphere (God) at any time, but we see a human being (a circle; John 1:18). The circles on the piece of paper are in a flat, two-dimensional plane. We see God in our terms. So it is God coming down to us, into our world of fewer dimensions. Perhaps the Spirit could then be seen as the continuity factor which joins the infinite numbers of circles into a picture – namely, the story of Jesus.

*Psychological analogy*
There are a number of psychological approaches that Western churches have developed in order to try to describe the Trinity. The ego, the id and the superego ('the ideal me') is a popular one; the ego, the unconscious id and the superego representing three parts, or egos, of the whole. We owe those concepts, of course, to Freud. Then again, those three centres of awareness operate within the Godhead as, perhaps, the mind, the intuition (emotion) and the will. There is also the mind, the knowledge and the will; or the mind, the knowledge and love; being, knowledge and love; and, finally, memory, intellect and will.

These six are all areas of awareness, or centres of awareness, that need to be properly integrated in a well balanced person, and they have been used to illustrate a unity in a diversity. If we meditate on them, they can help us to grasp the unity of a triune God.

*Agapetical analogy*
This is a terrible home-made word stemming from the Greek word *agape*, meaning love. This analogy utilizes the primacy of eternal love – lover, loved and love. Love always seeks to create

a unity without trying to destroy the individuality. That is what God is like; therefore, that is what the Church is meant to be like. The Father is seen as the Lover, and the Son as the Beloved in the spiritual bonding and magnetism of the Spirit, who is Love itself.

### *Philosophical analogy*
Since we experience personality and personhood (even though that word meant something more like a legal entity in the Early Church), it would not be surprising to find that God is experienced as a sort of supra-natural being. Because the source of a river is always higher than anything further down, we who are further down the river of creation experience personhood in a less intense way. The most important thing for us to know is that we are 'us' and not somebody else. Therefore, within the Godhead, it would be surprising if there wasn't something that relates to our experience of personhood, but it would probably be greater, so we call it three persons in one. God is the suprapersonal source of personhood, of which we are a lower experience. The source would contain all that humans are, only *more* so.

### *Theological analogy*
We have mentioned the Islamic trinity. We are always driven back to some plurality, no matter how monotheistic or monarchical we want to be, in order to explain all of our rich experience of life in this world of variety. If God is multi-relational, His creation will be, as well. Some sort of trinity is necessary to account for this diversity, as even the Koran recognizes.

### *Relational analogy*
Life is defined in biology and in botany in terms of the ability to give to and take from the environment. So, in Scripture, eternal

life that is God's is defined as knowing God and even Jesus Christ (John 17:3). The life of the eternal Father is called the eternal Son (1 John 1:1–4). There must be relationships for life to exist – even God's life. Therefore, there are the three relationships of the Godhead.

### Universal analogy
There is a diversity and a unity in the Creator, because the *uni*verse (uni = one) has diversity within it, reflecting the Creator.

### Experiential analogy
We saw this experiential analogy in chapter one. We experience God over us, God with us and God in us, and these relate to the three persons of the Trinity – dominion, communion, possession.

### Anthropomorphical analogy
Scripture defines humans as body, soul, and spirit (1 Thessalonians 5:23). It is highly probable that humans made in God's image might reflect or express something of the Trinitarian God. We see the Son of God, so He is like the body; and the Father's soul is revealed or empowered by the Spirit.

### Reflectorial analogy
There is the image of God: Jesus. This is made real by the light of the Spirit. As God looks in the mirror, He sees His image because the light carries from one to the other. (Perhaps the mirror itself could be one with the reflection, and this would be the Son of God.) This is obviously somewhat similar to the idea of the impersonal love that binds the lover and the loved one (see also Agapetical Analogy, above). The light is essential for the mirror

image, just as the object being reflected by the image is necessary. So the Father and the Spirit are necessary in order for the Son – the image of the invisible God (2 Corinthians 4:4; Colossians 1:15) – to be seen.

### Theatrical analogy

The playwright (the Father) conceives of a play; the actor (the Son) expresses it and acts it out, reveals it, brings it out of the author's mind into the 'real' world, so that we are able to see what is in the mind of the author. But the high point of ecstatic emotion occurs when the audience enters into the life that He is expressing, and on the stage the Son sees the impact of His words operating, and the Father's face is revealed by the Son. The Son's face is revealed by the Spirit; He takes the things of Christ and reveals them to us. But the Spirit's face (have you noticed how the Spirit always hides himself, always prays behind the scenes?) is seen in the audience. We see the face of the Spirit in each other – where the Spirit's face is revealed in the audience's looks and response. That is another Trinitarian analogy – the analogy of, if you like, 'the theatrical faces'.

### Heliological analogy

*Helios* is the Greek word for sun. The Father, the sun, is only seen by the light of the Son, and felt by the heat of the Spirit. If you look at the sun, you have to use its light and you will feel its heat. So we use the Son and Spirit in order to know the Father.

### Fluvial analogy

Another interesting analogy comes from Anselm, an archbishop of Canterbury in the eleventh century. He spoke about the Nile (including, perhaps, the river bank). With the ancient desire to find the source of the Nile we travel through the river and we keep going, remaining within its limits because the bank keeps us in – and eventually we find the source. That is how we know that there is a river there, because we have looked at the mouth of it – Jesus. We have seen its banks and its shape, and that is Jesus. As we travel along the water, which is the Spirit, we are held in, as it were, by the Son, until we find the source. That is coming to the Father, by the Son, through the Spirit.

### *Trisagional analogy*

This word is from Isaiah 6 and Revelation 4, and it means 'Holy, Holy, Holy' – that is, three 'Holies'. Now, let's suppose (to use a famous classical analogy) there are three chairs. So the concept of chair is there – 'chair concept', we might say – but there are three of them, and you have a 'oneness' and a 'tripleness' in that. Similarly, 'Holy, Holy, Holy' seems to represent the persons of the Godhead in their separateness (holy means 'separated from'), and yet also in their unity (holy also means 'separated to'). There are many 'doublings' of words in Scripture, emphasizing intensity, but this is the only triple, and it is in the context of worship – the three are worshipped as one, yet distinctly.

### *Ornithological analogy*

There are three birds in Scripture representing the members of the Trinity. And the fascinating thing is that they are never confused; each bird always represents the same member of the Trinity. The Father is seen as the eagle, nesting right up in the eyrie which humans cannot reach. He is in heaven, carries the young on his wings (Deuteronomy 32:11) and teaches them how to fly and move around in faith. The Son refers to Himself as a hen in Matthew 23:37, saying to Jerusalem:

How often I wanted to gather your children together,
the way a hen gathers her chicks under her wings, and
you were unwilling.

The hen remains on the earth. And the Spirit is seen as the dove (Matthew 3:16). The dove was the first-century pet that went right into the home. The hen doesn't, the eagle doesn't, but the Spirit goes right into the home, and so the dove is there, right in our heart, in our breast.

To try to understand the Trinity is an amazing challenge that, by definition, is greater and beyond even our deepest thought. Therefore we have to acknowledge that, in some way, we are limited. But that should not stop us from enquiring, because we love our God. I hope that these analogies, even in this brief form, will help us to gain a deeper knowledge and understanding of the Lord as we think and meditate upon them.

# 9

# Trinitarian Worship

In describing God whom we worship, we could sum up our problem like this. Have you ever tried to describe the smell of coffee? You cannot really do it. We have a similar problem in dealing with the Trinity. We can analyse coffee, and describe it in various ways, but then we can also experience it by drinking – and, of course, we know it has a delightful smell. But to describe the smell adequately (or, for that matter, the taste) is virtually impossible. In the same way, we have been using words to investigate the personal source of all things, the Almighty God, the Maker of heaven and earth. It is therefore not surprising that we are still left with some mystery regarding the persons of the Godhead that defies being pinned down neatly and definitively. We have been dealing with something awe-inspiring, wonderful and worshipful. In the end, the depths of the Godhead are only plumbed by worship.

A song begins to run through our spirits – it is the song that emanates from a God who looks over His creation and, in particular, looks over us, and with joy sings in His love and captures our hearts. It is that kind of God that is the Trinitarian God whom we worship. We enter into something that exists in His own being that is analogous to worship, for God Himself is in a continuous vibration and movement of internalized loving adoration among the three persons of the Godhead. I want us to enter into that – because that is where we really begin to worship the Living God; the One who rejoices over us, also, 'with singing' (Zephaniah 3:17, NIV).

Why a chapter entitled Trinitarian worship? Is it merely a modern fad to raise both the issue of the Trinity and that of worship? Let me quote the British Council of Churches, an ecumenical body incorporating evangelical, liberal, charismatic and conservative streams. This is the statement they made, just a few years back, as they sought to alert the church in this nation to the seriousness of our situation as regards worship:

> The difference between the life and death of Christian worship depends on the recovery of Trinitarian worship.

It is no fad. If an organization in touch with the whole spectrum of church movements in Britain has made a statement like the above, we should take note. There has been, and with good reason (as we have been discussing), a revival of seeking to understand in greater depth the meaning of the Trinitarian God – God the Father, God the Son, God the Holy Spirit. The Trinitarian emphasis is being resurrected, and surely this is the Spirit of God bringing the Church back to consider truth afresh and deeply. I pray and I long that that day would arrive when interest in the triune God is so vital that, just as in the time of the Cappadocian fathers, we are all discussing it again. I long for the day when, just as in those days, it is the subject of conversation at the baker's and at the gym, in the launderettes and when going through the supermarkets forgetting what we are buying, because we are so caught up with this wonderful God who made the heavens and the earth. Aren't you interested in Him? Don't you want to know the depths of His being?

Well, this knowledge really comes about not just by a cool, calm and calculated conversation about the Trinity, but actually in the mystery of worshipping this most majestic and wonderful being. This is nothing novel – lovers of God have known it through the centuries:

> Holy, holy, holy! Lord God Almighty!
> Early in the morning our song shall rise to thee;
> Holy, holy, holy, merciful and mighty!
> God in three persons, blessed Trinity!

Reginald Heber wrote this in the nineteenth century. And, again, Edward Cooper (1770–1833):

> Father of Heaven whose love profound
> A ransom for our souls hath found,
> Before Thy throne we sinners bend;
> To us Thy pardoning love extend.

> Almighty Son, incarnate word,
> Our Prophet, Priest, Redeemer, Lord,
> Before Thy throne we sinners bend;
> To us Thy saving grace extend.

> Eternal Spirit, by Whose breath
> The soul is raised from sin and death,
> Before Thy throne we sinners bend;
> To us Thy quickening power extend.

> Jehovah – Father, Spirit, Son –
> Mysterious Godhead, Three in One,
> Before Thy throne we sinners bend;
> Grace, pardon, life to us extend.

It is worth noticing at this point that, as many hymns express and the creeds assert, the Christian Church through the centuries has addressed, in prayer, song and worship, all three members of the Godhead – including the Holy Spirit. This seems quite natural to us but, strangely, there actually is no clear example of addressing the Spirit in Scripture. Two examples in types can be found. Ezekiel 37:9 shows God commanding the prophet to speak to the breath, or four winds, which of course is the Spirit ('spirit' and 'breath' being the same Hebrew word) of God. And, in Numbers 21:17, the water in the well is addressed in song, 'Spring up, O well!' This, of course, is another figure of the Holy Spirit. The Church has always recognized not only the Trinitarian God, but also our need to be able to *worship* Him: Father, Son *and* Holy Spirit. And this is our final subject, as well as our ultimate object: to worship the triune God in a Trinitarian way. As the Nicene Creed states and as Christians have done throughout history, we address the Holy Spirit, who 'together with the Father and the Son is worshipped and glorified'.

### Jesus and the Feast of Tabernacles

In John chapters 7 and 8, Jesus brings us two great revelations to do with Trinitarian worship. He does this, perhaps surprisingly, from within the context of the Jewish worship of His day. In chapter 7, Jesus goes up from Galilee to Jerusalem, to the Feast of Tabernacles (or 'Booths'), to join in the worship there. This great feast is described to us in the Jewish Talmud, and we shall look in a moment at the events that happened during the feast and at how Jesus uses them to show us more about the Trinitarian God whom we worship.

The Jews of Jesus' day were not, obviously, consciously Trinitarian. But it is clear from the rabbinical literature that the

Jews recognized from certain passages in the Old Testament that there was God, and then there was the Spirit that came from God, and that there was a distinction between the two. They also saw that there were places where the word of God was personified and was interacting in their lives. There was also the angel of the Lord, who consistently took on the functions of deity. The 'glory' of the Lord begins to be distinct from God and appears in the form of His fire, of a cloud and as a man; so too with God's name, and His Wisdom. The Jews were discussing these things around the time of Jesus and some, at least, were grappling with these distinctions and the way in which they saw God.

I want to suggest that when the Jews *worshipped*, they began to experience the triune God even though they did not have, as yet, a complete vocabulary to express it. They became really excited as they touched into the real, living God, as we shall see as we turn our attention now to the Feast of Tabernacles.

Theologians are agreed that this passage in John 7 involves the rite of water-drawing that took place on each of the seven days of the festival. The pilgrims, many of whom had come from far away to be part of the feast, entered into the procedures with great delight. Let me quote from the Talmud (*Tractate Sukka* 5.1), where the events of this great feast are recorded. It states that 'He who has not seen the joy of the water-drawing has not seen joy in his whole lifetime'. (For the background information on this feast, I am indebted to George Beasley-Murray's commentary on John, in the Word Biblical Commentary series (pp. 113ff and 127ff).

What would happen is that, at the break of day, priests would go in procession from the temple to the Pool of Siloam, where they would fill a golden pitcher with water. This they bore back again to the temple, and as they approached the water gate the shofar (trumpet) was sounded three times – three great and joyous blasts which echoed Isaiah 12:3:

> You will joyously draw water
> From the springs of salvation.

Then, as the pilgrims watched, the priests processed around the altar, bearing the water, while the temple choir sang the Hallel (Psalms 113–8). This took a little while! When they reached the first verse of Psalm 118, 'Give thanks to the Lord', every man and boy held aloft a citrus fruit in his left hand, as a sign of the harvest, and waved branches with his right, and shouted, 'Give thanks to the Lord!' three times. And when they reached verse 25, 'O Lord, save us!', they did the same thing again.

All of this happened at the time of the daily offering, and so when the drink offering of wine was offered to God, the water was offered along with it. Two silver bowls stood on the altar – one for the wine and one for the water. A chosen priest then climbed up onto the altar and poured the wine and water into their respective bowls; and then they were poured out as drink offerings to the Lord. The crowd cried, 'Lift up your hand!' and the priest did so, to show that he had fulfilled his duty.

The ideas behind this rite were somewhat complex, but they referred in part to the water that flowed from the rock that Moses had struck when the Israelites were in the wilderness and close to perishing from thirst (Exodus 17:1–6). There God had miraculously provided for them and saved them. We have already seen the link to Isaiah 12:3 regarding the springs of salvation. They also quoted from Ezekiel 47:1–12, which speaks of the water that will flow from the temple in Jerusalem, and Zechariah 14, where the water was going to burst forth as the Mount of Olives split in two. Thus, they looked to the salvation of God, past, present and future, and especially to the day when the kingdom of God would come and living water would flow from Jerusalem and refresh the souls of the people of God.

On the seventh day, the priests went back and forth seven times – seven times processing around the altar with the water from the Pool of Siloam. The excitement in the crowd was colossal. The festivities had already been going on all day for six days. But if these activities had been wearing them out in the daytime, they were not content with that! They went on into the night, and the really spiritual ones among them tried to last the entire seven days without sleep. And then, in the midst of this, possibly at the very moment when the priest held up his hand after pouring out the water, Jesus cries out:

> If anyone is thirsty, let him come to Me and drink. He who believes in Me, as the Scripture said, 'From his innermost being shall flow rivers of living water' (John 7:37–8)

He takes up the symbols of the festivities and expounds them, saying in effect: *The one who believes in Me, he will quench his thirst and will know a satisfaction that, even in this wonderful way you have been worshipping, you haven't found yet.* Jesus is beginning to expound what had been going on for the seven days in the water-drawing. He is explaining that if there is any joy in it at all – and indeed, many of them thought it was the greatest joy they had ever experienced – it was because the Spirit of God was to be poured out like water and they were enjoying His presence, His closeness, His intimacy only by anticipation as it ran down their throats into the very depths of their inner beings. God was there in the pouring of the water.

Verse 39 goes on to say:

> This He spoke of the Spirit, whom those who believed
> in Him were to receive; for the Spirit was not yet given,
> because Jesus was not yet glorified.

And when Jesus was glorified, the Spirit of the glorified Man who is also the Spirit of God was poured out upon the people. It is terribly important that we try and think of what is actually happening in our worship – the closeness of God and the closeness of the perfected Man who is now in the heavens are brought to us and into us by the Holy Spirit, and pour into our experience as we open up and give room through worship for the activity of God's water, God's Spirit.

That is the first great revelation that Jesus brings out for us from this festival. The second we find in John 8. To put it in context, let us find out what was happening during the nights of this amazing festival that Jesus was attending. Let me quote again from the description given in *Tractate Sukka* 5.1:

> Towards the end of the first day of the Feast of the Tabernacles, people went down into the court of the women, where precautions had been taken [to separate the men from the women]. Golden lamps were there, and four golden bowls were on each of them, and four ladders were by each; four young men from the priestly group of youths had jugs of oil in their hands containing about 120 logs [a log is a measurement of oil] and poured oil from them into the individual bowls. Wicks were made from the discarded trousers of the priests and from their girdles. There was no court in Jerusalem that was not bright from the light of the place of drawing [water]. Men of piety and known for their good works danced before them [the crowd] with torches in their hands, and sang before them songs and praises. And the Levites

stood with zithers and harps and cymbals and trumpets and other musical instruments without number on the 15 steps, which led down from the court of the Israelites into the court of the women and which corresponded to the 15 songs of the steps in the psalms.

It must have been an incredible sight. The whole of Jerusalem was lit up from these four great lamps that were burning in the courts of the temple, and the celebrations carried on each night of the festival. The fifteen songs that were sung on the fifteen steps were the fifteen Psalms of Ascent (Psalms 120–34). The dancing went on, night after night, before the Lord. Why did they do that? They had to, for they were touching a God who not only pours out water, as they were symbolizing by day, but a God who shines light that dances as beams and rays into every area of His universe; so much so that they had to move with that God and to dance with Him, because God was alive and vibrant in their midst.

One such dancer was Simeon, the son of Gamaliel, and he was renowned in these seven days of festivities. He had the ability to hold, yet throw in the air, four torches with each hand, and as those flames were burning, and as he danced before the Lord, it caused excitement. It was a kind of entertainment and a celebration all wrapped up together. This was worshipping Yahweh, the *Living* God. It wasn't worshipping some dead idol; nor was it worshipping themselves because they wanted some kind of freakish experience; it was the worship of the Living God in whom they delighted. It was dancing and singing because God dances and sings.

And the great torches that were sending light throughout the city of Jerusalem reminded the people of the fire of God's glory found in His cloud, which had led them from Egypt by night and by day. At the end of each night, two priests with trumpets would descend the steps to the place where the wonderful torches were burning. They would turn round and look towards the altar to show that they weren't worshipping the sun that was beginning to rise behind them; and they would cry out, 'We direct our eyes to the Lord!' They were saying: *We want the God who is the light of the universe.* Now Jesus in that context stands and says: 'I am the light of the world!' And so He speaks into the anticipatory, experiential Jewish worship of the triune God, which they did not yet fully understand. They were beginning to long for water; they were beginning to long for light. They wanted to know the Spirit and they wanted to know the Son of God, who is the light of the world and who gives understanding of the God whom we worship.

Jesus is putting into that worship at the Feast of the Tabernacles a theology that is going to help us, for the next two thousand years, to understand the worship of the triune God. We need His water of the Spirit. We need the Son's light shining and giving us understanding, in order that we might approach and know the Father. Jesus himself anticipates this New Testament triune worship. In Luke 10:21

> [*Jesus*] rejoiced greatly in the *Holy Spirit*, and said, 'I praise You, *O Father*, Lord of heaven and earth, that You have hidden these things from the wise and intelligent and have revealed them to infants.'

Jesus takes Jewish worship and shows that it is the Father being approached, but through the knowledge of the Son, who shines His light, and through the experience of the Spirit, whose closeness and nearness and presence make God's face very real.

If we ourselves have tasted something of this, then we will long for more. Then perhaps if we try to understand its meaning more deeply, it will lead us ultimately into greater and greater knowledge of God.

Finally, just before we leave this visit of Jesus to the Feast of Tabernacles, let us look at one of the Scriptures that we mentioned were read out during the feast. Zechariah 14:4 tells us: 'In that day His feet will stand on the Mount of Olives'. We see Jesus, the real incarnate God, with His feet put down in a real world. We, too, are going to put our real, solid feet down, because the resurrection is real and solid. The passage goes on to say:

> It will be a unique day which is known to the LORD, neither day nor night, but it will come about that at evening time there will be light. And in that day living waters will flow out of Jerusalem, half of them toward the eastern sea and the other half toward the western sea . . . And the LORD will be king over all the earth. (Zechariah 14:7–9)

When the kingdom comes, the living waters will flow forth; when the kingdom comes, the light of eternity will be shining, outshining the sun and the night. The trouble is, most of us are living on the wrong side of the kingdom. We are still looking forward to it, and so we hope that one day, when Jesus comes again, it will suddenly be there. But if we are born again, we can enter into it now through this kind of worship, which is open to every born-again believer. Jesus has adequately prepared and led the way, and we can know His light and life, both now and in the age to come.

## Problems with non-Trinitarian worship

### Monistic

If we do not worship the triune God, what are the alternatives? One is that we worship the monistic god that we discussed earlier, the 'God' who is the soul of the universe, the spirit that is everything, of whom we say the 'universe is god'. The problem with this is that we are a part of the universe, too, so we start worshipping ourselves also.

There is a certain degree of self-satisfaction and self-worship that can grow even in so-called Christian worship. We sometimes use sexual love as an analogy of loving God in worship – the Song of Solomon, for instance, is often understood that way. But we know how easily physical love can simply be a selfish sexual experience and nothing to do with giving pleasure to another. Similarly, worship can become a pursuit for our own satisfaction, without any real recognition that there is another person there – God – to receive from us, and who is wanting the best for us.

Monistic worship, or nature worship, is not Trinitarian Christian worship, although there may be times (but not for very long) when we might confuse the two. When those powers of nature are raised to a heightened level of experience, it is nature worship, monistic spiritual experience, but it is not worship of the triune God.

### Deistic

On the other hand, we could try to worship a god who is like that of the Muslims or Deists – a god who is sole and alone, distant, unapproachable and utterly 'other'. The trouble with worshipping this kind of transcendent god is that he seems to be demanding, 'Give me your worship', and thus sounds egocentric. Some Christian teaching sounds a bit like that, too. The Westminster Confession says that the chief end of humankind is to glorify God for ever. But why should God want us to worship and glorify Him for ever? There are many people who have reacted and objected to the Christian, the Jewish or the Muslim God, as being there solely waiting for adoration, as though he is infatuated with his own self-worth and needs the admiration of those around him. That is not triune worship, although a lot of people think it is. They see worship as trying to persuade God to think well of them and, further, they think: *Maybe if I do a little bit more worship, God might do something for me, give me some new sort of benefit in life, because I have worshipped Him.* Are they giving Him worship, or is it closer to flattery?

Triune worship, on the other hand, opens up the relations that exist within the Godhead and welcomes us in, so that we begin to capture in our own hearts and lives who He is. He wants us to worship because this is the way in which He can give us Himself, He who is the best of everything. He is not saying, 'Stand over there and worship Me', but rather: *Come in here and take Me, and have Me, and enjoy Me, because that is your true destiny.* That is what we were made for, to share eternal life; and where do we get eternal life, except from the Eternal One? Come in and enjoy what the Father, Son and Spirit are enjoying in the Godhead! This God is in a perpetual dance, as the Early Church fathers describe it, the *perichoresis* that we saw in chapter three. As they dance and move around one another, the Father into the Son, and the Son into the Spirit, and the Spirit moving to the Father, and as they are giving way to one another in that dynamic, eternal life, they say, *I want you, too, to have eternal life – worship your way in! The best thing for you is to worship Me, and so to be caught up in Me.*

This is eternal life – to know God, even Jesus Christ whom He has sent (John 17:3). And when, between the Father and the Son, by the power of the Spirit, we begin to engage in the movements, the heartbeat and the dynamic of a God who has been eternally enjoying Himself, because they are enjoying one another, we too experience eternal life. The Father is selflessly enjoying the Son; the Son selflessly enjoying the Spirit; the Spirit selflessly enjoying the Father. *Come and enjoy this selfless, self-giving dance of life! I made you for the dance*, says God, *may I have the pleasure? Although it is for your fulfilment, not Mine.* Surely God does not want masses of creatures to stand gawping at Him, saying, 'Oh, aren't you a magnificent God.' As though He needed such a thing! He has it already anyway, because the Father admires the Son, and the Son admires the Father, and the Father admires the Spirit. The Spirit says, *Come and join us, enter in*, and the Bride, the Church, also says, *Come* (Revelation 22:17).

## Greek philosophy

There is another potential problem with worship: if we impose too much Greek philosophy on the Bible, God becomes impassible – emotionless, unable to feel anything. In this view, God cannot change, cannot feel, is unmovable. Notice that these are all negative words. We have already considered the unmoved Aristotelian God, and seen that not only is such a God unable to engage in a relationship with us, but he would never dance. That is why we need a triune God, because the definition of perfection is not: 'if you change today, you could not have been perfect the day before'. Rather, it is in terms of *relationship*, and Father, Son and Holy Spirit are in a perfect relationship for all eternity. That is perfection. There is movement and dynamic in that perfection – which is far from the dead, cold, unmovable marble 'god' of Aristotelian theology.

In the action and in the life of movement is perfection. The changeability – the ability to change (though not in character), the ability to take, the ability to give way to one another – that's life. It is that kind of God who, as we worship Him, gives us His eternal life.

**Trinitarian worship**

Trinitarian worship takes *relationships* and *life* thoroughly into account (John 17:3). Furthermore, it begins to undo where sin began in not giving glory to God, and in being ungrateful, and then finally in being abandoned from God's presence (Romans 1:20–4). We recover when we start to glorify, and to give thanks. We open ourselves up for Him to give Himself to us as we give ourselves to Him, and His presence returns: take not your *Spirit* from me, nor remove your *face* from me. The Spirit and the face of God are paralleled twice in the Old Testament, in Psalm 51:11 and 139:7 (the Hebrew word sometimes translated 'presence' has, as its primary meaning, 'face'), and most apparently in the New Testament in 2 Corinthians 3:17–4:6. The presence of the Spirit makes God's closeness and nearness – His face – evident in our lives.

If we are honouring the Father and giving thanks to the Son, then we are taken up by the presence of the Spirit for communion, closeness, nearness and fellowship. Ephesians 2:18 says that we have access in the Spirit, through the Son, to the Father. Again, here the persons of the Godhead are engaging with us *in the Spirit*. It is also by His power and activity through the Son that He gives the revelation, 'He who has seen Me has seen the Father' (John 14:9). Thus, we are brought to the Father, through the Son, in the Spirit.

Now, in John 17, in the upper room, the singing and dancing is going on – at least they sing the Hallel (Psalms 113–8). Jesus stands up, and it is a special sort of dance. He has done the washing of feet, that is a kind of a dance; but then, in prayer, He takes the disciples in His arms and implies, *Father, I accept those that you gave me, I have revealed to them Your holy name, Father, as You asked Me to do; that was the mission, righteous Father.* As He talks to the Father He puts His arms around the disciples, by the Spirit (the arm of God). Thus, the disciples are in the Spirit, and they are coming through the Son to access the Father. And they are listening to the heartbeat of the communion of deity. Father to Son, Son to Father. They are almost, we could say, in between the conversation – not perhaps butting in, because they are too awe-inspired to speak. They don't say a word in John 17. They are simply drawn in between the Father and the Son, as the Father and the Son talk together.

This is life eternal: to know God and to know Jesus Christ. Through the Son becoming incarnate, we have the possibility of coming between the communion of the First and the Second Persons of the Godhead – gathered in by the Third Person of the Godhead, the Holy Spirit. That is where we are engaging. We may not say anything at all. We may be caught up in the song that is going on between the Father and the Son, but yet we may have to say something, and they don't mind – that's worship!

Hebrews 2:12–3 shows Jesus saying:

> 'I will proclaim Your name to My brethren,
> In the midst of the congregation I will sing Your praise.'

> And again, 'I will put My trust in Him.'

> And again, 'Behold, I and the children whom God has given Me.'

Jesus quotes Psalm 22 and Isaiah 8 here. Death and resurrection have taken place in this Psalm (see also verses 1 and 21); and so, by resurrection, Jesus stands in the midst of the Church, and there He sings praises to God, He reveals the name of the Father and He reasserts His faith and His commitment to His Father. This is where you can pick up a lot of faith! Get between the faith that Jesus had, and the Father, when He said, 'I will put my trust in Him, I and the children that You have given Me', quoting from Isaiah. He is in the congregation, in the Church, in the midst of us, and as He puts His faith in His Father, and we get caught up in the conversation, we can say, *Yes, I too can trust You, Father!*

Paul's blessing in 2 Corinthians 13:14 is that we may know and live in

> the grace of the Lord Jesus Christ, and the love of God,
> and the fellowship of the Holy Spirit.

We enter into the will and purpose of God, and into sharing eternal life, by worshipping within the eternal song and dance of the Godhead, who is always moving, interacting and sharing; who is always engaging and going in and out of each one of our lives. He picks us up as we begin to share in this and, incredibly, He takes us around in the dance, and sings over us (Zephaniah 3:17) – so much so that we want to dance with each other as well. We all want to share in each other's lives and to let the love of God flow out, because we have worshipped and are worshipping. Then we begin to bless one another, and share with each other, and bring answers to prayer for each other and find grace for each other – because that is what our God has done for us and is still doing for us.

We have got a triune God to worship. Let's worship Him for the love that He is Himself. That love has chosen a will for our lives: *Hear, O Israel! The LORD our God is one God; Him only shall we serve. And you shall love the LORD your God with all your heart and with all your soul and with all your might, with all your strength.* That is how, having loved Him in worship, we can go out and love our neighbour as ourselves, in the overflow of His love and in the worship of the song and dance of the Trinity.

# Epilogue

The Trinitarian prayer of St Patrick shows us the historic, orthodox Church commitment to the unique God of Christian revelation. Let us worship with him:

I bind unto myself today
The strong Name of the Trinity,
By invocation of the same
The Three in One and One in Three.

I bind this day to me for ever
By power of faith, Christ's incarnation;
His baptism in Jordan river,
His death on Cross for my salvation;

His bursting from the spicèd tomb,
His riding up the heavenly way,
His coming at the day of doom
I bind unto myself today.

I bind unto myself the power
Of the great love of cherubim;
The sweet 'Well done' in judgement hour,
The service of the seraphim,

Confessors' faith, Apostles' word,
The Patriarchs' prayers, the Prophets' scrolls,
All good deeds done unto the Lord
And purity of virgin souls.

I bind unto myself today
The virtues of the starlit heaven,
The glorious sun's life-giving ray,
The whiteness of the moon at even,

The flashing of the lightning free,
The whirling wind's tempestuous shocks
The stable earth, the deep salt sea
Around the old eternal rocks.

I bind unto myself today
The power of God to hold and lead,
His eye to watch, His might to stay,
His ear to hearken to my need.

The wisdom of my God to teach,
His hand to guide, His shield to ward;
The word of God to give me speech,
His heavenly host to be my guard.

Against the demon snares of sin,
The vice that gives temptation force,
The natural lusts that war within,
The hostile men that mar my course;

Or few or many, far or nigh,
In every place and in all hours,
Against their fierce hostility
I bind to me these holy powers.

Against all Satan's spells and wiles,
Against false words of heresy,
Against the knowledge that defiles,
Against the heart's idolatry,

Against the wizard's evil craft,
Against the death wound and the burning,
The choking wave, the poisoned shaft,
Protect me, Christ, till Thy returning.

Christ be with me, Christ within me,
Christ behind me, Christ before me,
Christ beside me, Christ to win me,
Christ to comfort and restore me.

Christ beneath me, Christ above me,
Christ in quiet, Christ in danger,
Christ in hearts of all that love me,
Christ in mouth of friend and stranger.

I bind unto myself the Name,
The strong Name of the Trinity,
By invocation of the same,
The Three in One and One in Three.

By Whom all nature hath creation,
Eternal Father, Spirit, Word:
Praise to the Lord of my salvation,
Salvation is of Christ the Lord.

(Translated from the Gaelic by Cecil F. Alexander)

# Bibliography

Barth, Karl, *Church Dogmatics* (Edinburgh: T&T Clark, 1956–75)

Erikson, Millard J., *Making Sense of the Trinity* (Grand Rapids, MI: Baker Book House, 2000)

*Forgotten Trinity, The* (London: Report of BBC Study Commission – Trinitarian Doctrine Today BBC, 1989)

Fretheim, Terrence E., *The Suffering of God* (Philadelphia: Fortress Press, 1984)

Gunton, Colin E., *The Promise of Trinitarian Theology* (Edinburgh: T&T Clark, 1991–7)

Knight, George A. F., *A Christian Theology of the Old Testament* (Carlisle: Paternoster Press, 1998)

McGrath, Alister, *Understanding the Trinity* (Eastbourne:Kingsway, 1987–99)

Moltmann, Jürgen, *The Trinity and the Kingdom of God* (London, SCM Press, 1981)

Pinnock, C. H., *The Flame of Love* (Downers Grove, IL: IVP, 1996)

Torrance, T. F., *The Christian Doctrine of God* (Edinburgh:T&T Clark, 1996)